OUR SCHOOLS

The Canadian Centre for Policy Alternatives

OUR SELVES

Our Schools / Our Selves is published four times a year by the Canadian Centre for Policy Alternatives, 410-75 Albert St., Ottawa, ON K1P 5E7. This is Volume 18, Number 2, Issue #94 of the journal (Winter 2009). *Our Schools / Our Selves* is a member of the Canadian Magazine Publishers Association. It is indexed in the Canadian Magazine Index and the Alternative Press Index.

EXECUTIVE EDITOR
Erika Shaker

EDITOR EMERITUS
Satu Repo

ASSOCIATE EDITOR
Larry Kuehn

ISSUE EDITOR
Jessica Yee

EDITORIAL OFFICE
Suite 410, 75 Albert Street, Ottawa, ON, K1P 5E7

SUBSCRIPTIONS AND ADVERTISING
Canadian Centre for Policy Alternatives, 410-75 Albert St., Ottawa, ON K1P 5E7 tel: (613) 563-1341 fax: (613) 233-1458

ISSN 0840-7339
ISBN 978-0-88627-544-0

PRODUCTION
Typesetting and design: Nancy Reid. Printed in Canada by Imprimerie Gagne, 750 Ave. Deveault, Louiseville, PQ J5V 1B4. Publications Mail Registration No. 8010.

Cover Illustration: Jennifer Yee
Cover Design: Nancy Reid (www.nrgrafix.com)
First Page: Poster design - Nadine Boyce/Photo - Jessica Yee

Contents

VOLUME 18, NUMBER 2 (#94) WINTER 2009

Yankton Sioux Nation

JESSICA YEE

Introduction

I have long wondered about the vast relationships between the sexual education youth of colour are receiving and the impact of colonization on their sexuality in general. As a First Nations young woman, I often hear about colonization and how it is has gravely affected the state of our people for generations on a multitude of levels, but rarely do these discussions go anywhere near the topic of sexuality. In my discussions with other youth of colour, more often than not I hear the same things being said, and the same exasperating results of this widespread reluctance to make sexual health a priority for all of our youth.

So is it any wonder that when approaching the subject of sexual education youth of colour are receiving in Canada, it is quite difficult to explain what exactly I'm looking for, and to find any resources that concretely address these very issues? I'm not looking for materials on how to be inclusive when teaching sex ed, and I'm certainly not looking for another adult to tell us as youth how we need to behave sexually. The information that is frequently disseminated from communities of colour regarding our sexual health is almost always pervasive in nature, highly statistical, and seldom speaks to the true realities we are facing to be represented in those "risky" numbers in the first place.

What happened to us anyway? Why is it that so many communities of colour are disproportionately affected to the point where many of us feel that we are, yet again, raising the importance of equitable sex education alone?

Colonization has a lot to do with that, and here in Canada we need to remember just how many of us are suffering the intergenerational impacts of colonization and what exactly it has done to us. Colonization is more than Columbus coming over to discover the "New World" in 1492 and causing the genocidal affect millions of Indigenous peoples throughout the world can still painfully feel. Colonization is still happening, and it didn't just happen to us as First Nations.

> *"Without taking full control of our lives, starting with our own bodies, we would simply be wards of the state". – Katsi Cook*

Before the invention of clinics, anatomy textbooks, or sexual health websites, my own people were practicing sexual education, living with the ideals of feminism, and utilizing theories of reproductive justice to live as a healthy, strong, autonomous nation.

We might not have called it sexual health, or labeled it with any sort of clinicized connotation, but we sure as hell have always believed in our rights over our own bodies, and how fundamental that is to our continued existence. I mean, what do people really think we used to do? Wait for the colonizers to come and teach us about sex?!

You would think however that we would get the recognition for starting the concepts and frameworks that many non-Native academic movers and shakers have been internationally hailed for, but alas, we do not. In fact my people have been so far removed from practicing our authentic ways that a lot of us don't even want to identify with any of our former sex-positive existence.

Sex was upheld in our culture as not only a sacred and powerful part of human life, but as a very normal part of it, too. Sexual education began in the ancient huts, longhouses, and teepees of our ancestors, where young people would learn from selected family or community members all about their body, how to care for it, and the inviolability of their sex. Many of our ancestral teachings show us that many of our societies were matriarchal and this included healthy, educated decisions over matters of childbearing and sexuality. We have different ceremonies and traditions that we've been practicing for centuries to back this up.

Our long history of genocidal oppression whether through colonization, Christianization, residential/mission/boarding schools, or just blatant racism has drastically severed the ties between us and how traditionally we might have received the knowledge that would enable us to make informed choices about our sexual health and relationships. The fact is that many of our communities are reluctant to go anywhere near the topic of sexual health because it is now viewed as "dirty", "wrong", or a "Whiteman's thing."

We have also carried a long history of being sexually exploited; which can be seen anywhere from the early Pocahontas and Squaw days right up until the modern over-sexualization of "easy" Native women, which still permeates much of the media.

> *"The American ideal of sexuality appears to be rooted in the American ideal of masculinity. This idea has created cowboys and Indians, good guys and bad guys, punks and studs, tough guys and softies, butch and faggot, black and white. It is an ideal so paralytically infantile that it is virtually forbidden — as an unpatriotic act — that the American boy evolve into the complexity of manhood." —James Baldwin*

We share this agonizing history with so many other communities of colour, whose Western World invaders (whether through forced Christianization or removal of nations into slavery), sought to take away one of our most powerful human abilities: our sexuality, and use it against us to control, destroy, colonize, and mould us into exactly what they wanted us to be. English, a confusing language which the dominant society here insists we still speak, has created binaries like gay and straight, supremacy and subservience, which many of our communities simply didn't subscribe to. We're more interested in the essence of our humanity.

It's definitely worth reflecting on how different things might be if our future generations know about where we came from and call on their ancestral roots to help them make it through these present-day oppressions that we face. I think our job now is to find practical ways to translate all of this into modern terms for our young people to use so they can recover what past generations may have lost, and re-assert themselves as the resilient, fierce, and knowledgeable young people who were, once upon a time, the most sacred in many of our cultures.

> *"Colonization and racism go hand in hand. Racism has provided justification for the subjugation of peoples ... Over time, racial stereotypes and societal rejection may be internalized by the colonized group."*
>
> *— Emma D. LaRocque*

We also must dispel the myth that Canada is a "mosaic" of cultures where everyone gets along in perfect racial symbiosis — and this is something our youth today need to be talking more about. While there might be multiple ethnicities, races, and cultures represented in larger urban centres like Toronto, Vancouver, Edmonton, and Montreal (and this only represents four cities of the 10 provinces and three territories in all of Canada), we aren't usually discussing how and why this is happening in order to facilitate knowledge, respect, appreciation and understanding. Toronto alone has more than 60,000 Aboriginal people according to the 2006 Stats Canada Census, but walking through the city streets you might never know who and where they are.

Growing up in the sprawling diverse metropolis of Toronto I hear people of colour say that while we might have neighbourhoods like Chinatown and Little Italy, we don't really sit down and discuss our cultures with one another. We see our cultures represented mostly in festivals or conferences, while in actuality we have the ability to do more than that. It's not enough to simply look at the foods and colours of people if you want to know about their culture, you have to understand wholly where the person comes from. It's about more than just their country of origin.

Examining cultural competency and sex education means using what we already have in our culture to empower our youth to lead healthy, strong lives, while intersecting it with our present day realities. SEX is still such a taboo topic in our society, when in fact it is the foundation of all humanity and is related to every social issue on some level. While we look to other existential issues to problem solve the various challenges our communities are facing, the time has come to bring it back to the basics and strengthen our identities right from the ground up.

Rather than continuing to allow people outside our communities dictate to us how to be "healthy", not actually involving us as youth on any sustainable level when working "for youth", and rarely disseminating anything in a culturally competent way, I decided to go directly to the source itself. For this issue of *Our Schools / Our Selves*, I asked youth of colour about their experiences with sex education and if colonization, in its many forms, affects how they view sexuality.

In this issue we hear from youth in words that are unfiltered, powerful, truthful, raw, radically self-aware and painful on a wide spectrum of topics they needed to share. We hear first accounts of being a newcomer to the country and the frighteningly new methods of sex education. We listen to the tales of being gay in a culture that condemns it today, but so many years ago accepted homosexuality. We are inspired by the many youth change agents who are putting forward the gifts and strengths they carry, confronting their history of colonization, and breaking new ground to continue the fight.

What I really heard while putting all of these tales together was a loud, resounding cry from many youth that they are ready and willing to talk about sex and while 90% of the drama in their own communities had to do with sex, they felt that existing hierarchies, power structures and authority figures stood in the way and incapacitated them from making positive change. It is fair to say that we are already paying the price for the inadequacy in organizations, institutions, and society in general to actualize youth leadership when it comes to sex education.

> *"Peer education means that young people gain more from an experience when they are actively involved ... [and] is a core premise of peer education and youth development. Research also suggests that programs for youth which are developed through a partnership of youth and adults may be highly effective in building youth people's skills and reducing their sexual risk-taking behaviors."*
>
> *— Advocates for Youth, Peer Education, Youth Development, and Youth-Adult Partnerships*

The Merriam-Webster dictionary defines self-determination as "free choice of one's own acts without external compulsion, and especially as the freedom of the people of a given territory to determine their own political status or independence from their current state." It is essential that youth of colour are given the right to self-determination when we talk about sexual education, and that we listen carefully to how we can support them to realize this in their own lives. If we believe in autonomy, sovereignty, and self-government over our own bodies, youth must also be allowed these rights. How this plays out, looks, and works will vary greatly from youth to youth, reality to reality, and community to community.

I believe what it boils down to is not only the importance of our right to self-determination, but knowing and reclaiming our history. While today's youth were not alive when the initial colonization happened, we are alive now, and indeed it's still happening. We may not have been able to choose what our ethnicity was going to be, but we can own it now and stand as allies with other communities of colour. We can work together in our common struggle for the autonomy to live as our authentic selves in the face of oppression and bigotry. We need to celebrate our rich heritages in peaceful solidarity so we all survive, while together honouring the ancestors who lived so courageously to give us those few bits of raw culture we cling to today.

Education is the key to affecting positive change. Equitable and intersectional sex education — this is how we are going to take back our self determination and put it out there as it once was, strong, sexy, powerful, and most of all, unapologetic of who we are.

JOHN HUPFIELD

Too Much Sex, Not Enough Education

Statistics Canada recently released its 2006 Census data and for the first time in recorded history the Aboriginal population was over the one million mark; 1,172,790 to be exact. Mathematically speaking, these numbers are increasing due to a rising average growth rate of 2.8% in 1996, 3.3% in 2001 and 3.8% in 2006, compared to the non-Aboriginal growth rate of 0.869%. The Aboriginal population is currently growing six times faster than the non-Aboriginal population. I'll say that again — for every one new non-Aboriginal Canadian, there are six new Aboriginal people.

With all these new tiny, shiny humans the average age of Aboriginal people is 27 years old; 13 years younger than the 40-year-old baby-boomer non-Aboriginal population. The conclusion could be this obvious: Native peeps are getting wet and sticky at increasingly higher rates than their non-native counterparts. This raises a question though. If all these pheromone-soaked people are getting down, is this necessarily a good thing?

Recent studies in the United States found that Aboriginal youth pregnancy rates (69 of 1,000) are higher than the national rate (49 of 1,000). Why the huge disparity in statistics? It could be due to lack of relevant programming. Approximately 57% of

Natives live in urban areas in the U.S. with Canada's numbers mirroring those figures at 54%. However, a lot of government support is still given to rural Native populations, leaving a significant service gap for specific populations such as urban Native youth. This can result in some outcomes that may or may not be completely welcomed, such as unexpected "bundles of joy."

Sarah Forbes-Roberts life's work is educating people about sex and healthy practices — she just happens to make a living doing it commercially. With over ten years as co-owner of the Toronto-based sex positive boutique and co-operative, Come As You Are, Forbes-Roberts has heard it all before. "People will come in and say, 'I have this weird question…' and I'm like, I've already heard that three times today," she laughs. "That's not so weird."

"Sexual health info is not easily accessible for all peoples" says Forbes-Roberts. At Come As You Are the focus is on creating a positive space for everybody to learn about sex. "No matter their ethnicity, mobility, or age… we work hard to address all those differences."

Largely due to a lack of awareness in mainstream society, the co-op tackles difficult issues around sex such as racism, stereotyping, discrimination and just plain ignorance, in an effort to improve people's attitudes. "Everyone [who comes to the store] gets talked to… and we give respectful answers," says Forbes-Roberts. The unfortunate thing is, shops like Come As You Are aren't commonplace throughout Canada and they generally cater to the more wealthy members of society, so their positive vibes and info does not reach the people who may be needing it most. Our people are not talking about where babies come from, how STIs are spread, and how to protect ourselves even when we assume we are in a committed relationship.

Sexual health information may be "out there" and available through certain clinics and social agencies but a problem remains. In many cases it quite simply isn't reaching people. "The problem is our native youth are not being educated properly at home," says Theola Ross "Our native communities view sex as a 'hush hush' issue."

Even worse, when youth do end up pregnant they often don't even know what services are available to support them. Kayla McCoy, a 19-year-old single mother of two, has to travel over one hour to access programs and support for her children in a culturally sensitive environment within Toronto, and that's only after she found out about the services through a friend. "They [Native agencies] should make billboards and advertise or something, because I never knew you could get diapers and baby food 'till I came down here."

From a group of students signing petitions to get free condoms in Charlottetown, PEI, to youth organizing themselves into committees and holding conferences, the young people of this generation are beginning to take ownership of the situations they face and are seeking answers. All across North America Native youth are speaking out about the same things. "Have somebody speak at a powwow...'cause that's where a lot of Native teens are. You could just talk to them; tell them to protect themselves. Pass out condoms or something," voiced one youth in a 2007 study on Aboriginal adolescent pregnancy.

> **"We help people find what their sexual choice is... by being extremely non-judgmental."**
>
> ***— Sarah Forbes-Roberts***

Sarah Forbes-Roberts would like to see a number of ideas become more mainstream. She notes that on top of sex being a taboo issue, some communities face even greater barriers. "As a store we have an anti-discrimination belief [but] there are so many racist stereotypes around sex." By working towards breaking down the negative stereotypes and attitudes towards sex the goal is to make people more comfortable with their sexuality. With increased comfort, people might actually feel like talking about it so they can begin making positive choices for themselves. Sarah adds, "We help people find what their sexual choice is... by being extremely non-judgmental." In doing this, Forbes-Roberts is effectively opening channels for learning as well as space for safe discussion and shared knowledge.

I think that the numbers can go down by a lot with education, but I don't think that's the only solution. Opening up a platform for casual conversations about sex and getting rid of the taboos in our culture would make an enormous difference. Everything from family, peers, media, society, work and school; influence our sexuality, gender roles, and sexual behaviors.

Out of all those influences our families and caregivers are always number one. We see sex as an area that just isn't discussable; otherwise we may be thought of as perverted or dirty. Since our youth are the backbone to our society, it is imperative that they get the tools necessary to make smart decisions regarding sex. Otherwise, the rates in our communities will stay the same or increase.

Our community has to change its thought process when it comes to sex/sexuality. Sexuality is fluid, natural, open, and normal (regardless of sexual preference) and it should be viewed that way. After figuring out that sex isn't some deep, dark secret, then we can branch off into educating ourselves. What needs to happen for this to improve? We have a culture that needs to stop stigmatizing, punishing, or socially ostracizing due to people's sexuality. ACCEPTANCE IS THE KEY TO IMPROVING.

Ojibway author and playwright Drew Hayden Taylor once said, "Our biggest secret is now out. Yes it's true. Indians do have sex." Is this always a good thing though? The problems are much more difficult and complex and throwing condoms at them won't make them go away, but at least now that it is out in the open things are in a position where they can begin to change for the better. Step one: listen to the youth of today, because they are speaking...

* * *

Anishinaabe filmmaker, writer, and community developer, ***John Hupfield*** *is from Wasauksing First Nation. Calling Toronto his home, where he is currently engaged as a youth worker, Hupfield also works to affect change using multi-media forms as a medium.*

BY JASMINE REDFERN
With contributions from ANNA SOOLE and DANIELLE GAULD

My Story
Colonization, sexuality and Aboriginal youth

Foreword

Imagine you are four years old, all you have ever known is the safety of your family, community, traditions and culture. One day strangers invade your home and take you by force to a place that is alien and hostile to you. You are forbidden to speak your own language, your traditions are stripped from you, and you are deprived of the care and nurturing of your family. You suffer neglect, physical, emotional, sexual and spiritual abuse.

Between 1840 and 1996 over 150,000 Aboriginal children endured the Residential School system in Canada. Operated by major religious authorities, these schools were endorsed as a tool of colonization by the Government of Canada in order to "Kill the Indian in the child." *

We as Aboriginal people have experienced and continue to endure a cultural genocide.

The 1948 United Nations Convention on the Prevention and Punishment of the Crime of Genocide defines genocide as "any of the following acts committed with intent to destroy, in whole or in part, a national, ethnical, racial or religious group, as such: killing members of the group; causing serious bodily or mental harm to members of the group; deliberately inflicting on the group conditions of life, calculated to bring about its physical destruction in whole or in part; ***imposing measures intended to prevent births within the group; [and] forcibly transferring children of the group to another group."*** *Throughout our lives we have heard innumerable accounts from Aboriginal women survivors of Residential Schools who endured surgical procedures that left them sterile without their prior knowledge or consent. There are even more accounts of sexual abuse and the shaming of sex and sexuality within the Residential School system. These realities coupled with the loss of our traditional languages, and no new words to replace our languaging around sex and sexuality, left us without any tools to assert or even negotiate our sexual rights, responsibilities or desires.*

This is the legacy we as Aboriginal youth today live with. Many of our families are still learning how to survive in a system that is designed to destroy us, there is little time or resources for them to think about how best to instill a sense of being unashamed, safe or even proud of our innate sexuality. The sense of shame and silence around sexuality that colonization has instilled in our communities leaves those of us who are just waking up to our sexuality hungry for information and vulnerable to misinformation.

As a young Aboriginal woman, my first experience with institutionalised sexual health education was in the 5th grade at Nakasuk Elementary School in Iqaluit, Nunavut. The school combined all the 5th and 6th grade classes and handed us little bags of condoms, tampons, a travel sized deodorant and a pamphlet about puberty. We got a brief talk about the changes our bodies would soon be going through but it was vague and none of us really listened because we were all busy playing with the contents of our goody bags. The instructor, who was in her late fifties, wasn't exactly the most engaging speaker when it came to understanding our bodies to say the least.

Sex wasn't really brought up again until 8th grade, our first year of high school. Our teacher was fun and enthusiastic but the material was still bland and lacking. We were shown the typical pictures of genitals with different infections and shown a condom demonstration. Then the unit was over.

I feel nothing that I learned in those classes prepared me for my life as a young sexual Aboriginal girl. The classes assumed that there was one way to have sex and that only straight people need to know about safer sex. They did nothing to teach me to be comfortable, let alone confident, talking about sex or building healthy sexual self esteem.

My first sexual encounter, and by this I mean my first kiss which was followed that same year with the first time I gave oral sex to a guy, was when I was eleven or twelve. Many of my classmates had already engaged in sexual acts and a handful of them were actively having sex. Nearly all of my peers were sexually active in middle school, years before we would actually learn anything about sex in school. The school system did not coincide with our reality. (According to a 2005 McCreary study 29% of Aboriginal youth are having sex before the age of 14, 19% more than the national average). We had no one to talk to. No one told me that there were ways I could be sexually confident without having sex or that I was allowed to decide when and with whom I would have sex. Sure, I knew I could say no, but I felt obligated and my male counterparts seemed to feel entitled.

I had no skills to navigate my sexuality. Girls in my class measured our self worth and status by how much attention we received from boys.

I had no skills to navigate my sexuality. Girls in my class measured our self worth and status by how much attention we received from boys. So when girls were uncomfortable we felt we had to ignore our intuition because we'd never been given the skills to understand our self worth without the drug of validation from boys. I had no idea how to assert myself when I was uncomfortable. I didn't even know what boundaries were, let alone how to identify and assert mine. All of my peers were so self-conscious and scared that we couldn't even talk to each other about how we felt or what was going on and even if we wanted to we wouldn't have had the language for it.

As youth, our roles in society are dictated to us. We're told we have no power, we're not allowed to vote and therefore not involved in politics, and we're even told what gender we are and what that is supposed to mean to us. Before colonization, gender roles in Aboriginal communities were fluid and situational. For example: it was typical that a boy would be raised to become a hunter. If a family only had a daughter she instead would be raised to be a hunter. In Aboriginal traditions, people who move fluidly through masculine and feminine, now called "two spirited" individuals, were often people

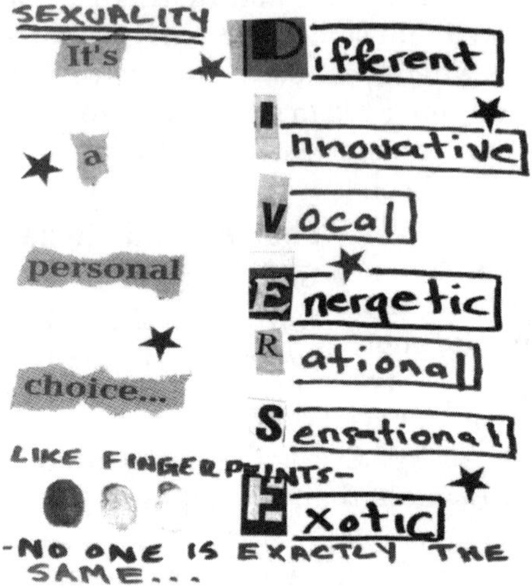

Black Queer Youth Initiative (BQY)

of elevated status, holding positions in the community such as healer, guide, prophet, and chief. There are few accounts of "two spirited" people being shunned or disapproved of prior to the point of contact between settlers and Aboriginals. Since contact, many tribes and individuals have adopted a sense of sexism, heterosexism, homophobia and transphobia which are colonized attitudes.

All of these issues related to my age and gender were also tangled up in my experience of being Aboriginal. As Aboriginals, we've been taught to hate ourselves by the colonizers for generations and many of us have internalized and perpetuated this attitude. During colonization, Aboriginal children were cut off from our families and taught to live as white people because it was assumed our way of life was wrong and "savage." We were taught to ignore our traditions, forget our languages, and lose our self identity. Subsequently, Aboriginals today and youth in particular struggle to be who we are and live a modern life in western society. With this comes a sense of uprooted-ness, disenfranchisement, and loneliness which can lead to pain and anxiety and puts Aboriginals at risk of engaging in coping behaviours and activities that could ultimately harm us. When our youth turn to drugs and alcohol, or engage in indiscriminate sexual behaviours it is often an attempt to fill the void left by the loss of our connection to Spirit, community and traditions. This puts us at a much higher risk of HIV (and other STI) infections than non-Aboriginal youth in Canada, (on average we are about three times more likely, according to the McCreary Centre Society).

I can't go back and give myself the knowledge or skills that I wish I would have had, but I can use my experience to share knowledge and engage my peers. And that's exactly what I am doing. I have learned that in order to develop a curriculum to effectively educate Aboriginal youth on sexual health there needs to be a marriage of western medical framework with holistic, culturally sensitive teachings. Traditionally Aboriginal peoples have practiced education through story telling and mentoring. A similar approach needs to be taken to sexual health education. It is important for programs to give information to youth on how to protect ourselves in a variety of situations, taking into consideration that most people are not made from cookie cutters. Aboriginal youth would benefit from sexual health education provided by someone with whom we can relate: an Aboriginal individual and ideally a youth, who has been through similar situations and who is comfortable talking frankly about sex.

This is exactly why three Vancouver-based organizations, YouthCO AIDS Society, Chee Mamuk and Healing our Spirit, have partnered to create the Aboriginal Youth Harm Reduction Project. Our project is a youth-driven, peer-based, culturally sensitive HIV/AIDS and Hep C prevention program. The project aims to engage youth in non-judgemental, peer led discussions to both explore what issues we as Aboriginal youth are facing and to arm ourselves with information and skills we have learned over our lifetimes. We then offer participants the opportunity to express what they have learned through an art project using traditional methods such as story telling, making medicine pouches, singing, drumming or beading and blending these mediums with modern methods such as creating claymation videos, hip hop music or using Forum Theatre. The goal is that through these workshops, which can vary from an hour and a half to several days, youth participants will have increased knowledge of risks associated with sex and sexuality and also know how to reduce the risk in their own lives, learning to channel the strong feelings that can come up during these conversations into something tangible. They will have an understanding of the emotional, spiritual, mental and physical elements of sexuality and will have opened the door for future discussion on sexuality and what it is that puts Aboriginal youth in the highest percentile for HIV infections in Canada.

* At the time that the Indian Act was created the term "Indian" was used as a blanket term for anyone indigenous to North America including First Nations, Inuit and Metis people.

* * *

Jasmine Redfern *is an Inuk youth from Iqaluit, Nunavut. She is the Outreach Educator for the Aboriginal Youth Harm Reduction Project at YouthCO AIDS Society in partnership with Healing Our Spirit and Chee Mamuk.*

Anna Soole *is a Metis youth and was raised in BC. She coordinates the Aboriginal Youth Harm Reduction Project and the Forum Theatre Troupe at YouthCO AIDS Society in partnership with Healing Our Spirit and Chee Mamuk.*

Jasmine Redfern and Anna Soole can be contacted at YouthCO AIDS Society at 604-688-1441 or www.youthco.org.

Danielle Gauld *is an ally for Aboriginal peoples. She manages the Sexual Health Program at YouthCO AIDS Society.*

Chee Mamuk *provides culturally-appropriate on-site community based HIV/AIDS and Sexually Transmitted Disease education and training to Aboriginal communities, organizations, and professionals within BC.*

YouthCO *is Canada's first youth-driven organization leading the HIV and HepC movement through peer education, support, and shared leadership.* ***Healing Our Spirit*** *is a BC-based Aboriginal-specific AIDS Service organization.*

DJ DANFORTH

"Kill the Indian, Save the Man"
A young Oneida man's perspective on sexuality

Many of the young men in the Native communities across Canada and the U.S. are in much need of traditional education about the right to express their sexuality and how to accept the nature of their sexuality. Colonization has certainly done its damage to our young men and not only is this affecting them, but the women and children of our communities as well. Present day, Western society's prevalent view of sexuality has negatively affected our young men. Western society seems to believe that sexuality is linear; where men should love women and women should love men. That is to say, men should only do "manly" things, and women should follow suit with their "womanly stuff".

This is not how it was traditionally for our people; we respected the way people existed sexually for themselves, and if, for example, someone in the community was Two-Spirited or homosexual, well then that meant they possessed some healing powers and that was respected in the community.

Today things have obviously changed and for the young men, there have been severe ramifications and long lasting effects across our nations. There has been a resurgence of programs that are women-centred and reach out to females for support, and while this is a good and necessary thing; we still have a long way to go until either sex gets the healing they need. However, there are definitely not a lot of programs out there for men that reach out to our young men specifically who are growing up in a colonial, sexist world. This is truly problematic, and I think we're seeing the effects of it in young men's ability to express their true sexuality and feel comfortable doing it.

Ever since the forceful enrollment of Native children in the 1800's into boarding and residential schools the learned behavior of the foreign world was forced upon our children into thinking that what was naturally right for us is actually wrong. The concept of these schools was to "kill the Indian, and save the man", and through these types of concentration camps they began to carry out this intention. These forced teachings have had long term effects on our people, and the victims began to live by what they were forcefully taught. This was principally out of fear that if they began to live the way their ancestors did, then they would have to go back to these schools or worse. I remember a time when my father asked my great grandmother why she didn't pass down traditions to his mother and him. She replied that she was scared that; "The soldiers would come back and take away her daughter and grandchildren" if they had learned the traditional way of life. These kinds of accounts are heard all over Turtle Island and through attending residential and boarding school, our way of expressing sexuality began to disappear and turn into what we see today.

When I was teaching in Marty, South Dakota for the past two years, I witnessed many young men who thought that the correct way to treat their companions was through various forms of domestic violence. When I asked them where they had learned this behavior, the response was somewhat disturbing. They said that they would see their father abuse their mother and for the young men it was a way to show love to their partners, since the example was modeled directly in their homes. Again, we hear stories like this in many of our communities, and the fact that there is not a lot being done to resolve these situations with our young people in mind is only making it acceptable to our youth. To think that youth today are raised believing it is okay to treat their companions with abuse is a very scary thing for our people.

As a young Native man who lives and works in the community, I have spent a lot of time reflecting on how men could do such things to women, and how they could honestly say that it was love they were expressing to their partners. Today I have set a standard for myself to help all young men of colour who are surviving colonization to educate and encourage them to express their true sexuality, and learn about the affects of domestic violence and abuse. Young men need to come back to the roots of their culture, and accept the fact that this is happening to our people everywhere, because then we can try and figure out how we as a nation can help make it stop. If young men can come to terms with the realities that are happening to our people and recognize that it's affecting our future generations, then that's the same unity and strength our ancestors possessed. This is not only for men but for the women too, because the women are so very important to us. Women should and deserve to be treated as sacred beings with love and respect to the greatest level possible.

* * *

DJ Danforth *is a proud 25-year-old Native young man from the Oneida Nation. He is currently the Youth Cultural Coordinator for the Oneida Tribe of Wisconsin, and sings with drum groups Elk Soldier, and Tha Tribe.*

Build a respectful workplace
Speak out with one voice
against racism, harrassment and prejudice
Make a real difference at work. Make a real difference in the world!
CAW TCA
CANADA
www.caw.ca

AGITATE

WWW.AGITATE.WORDPRESS.COM

Agitate is a queer, Ottawa-based organization for Aboriginal, mixed-race and women of colour. Although the governing board is open exclusively to First Nations, mixed-race and women of colour, allies from all communities and of all genders and sexual orientations are encouraged to get in touch with Agitate for information on how to volunteer.

Agitate's aim is to provide queer visibility within racialized and ethnic communities; outreach; social programming; education; transnational perspectives; and anti-racist activism. Agitate will also forge links with other organizations who share a similar vision of social justice. Agitate was borne out of recognition of the intersecting nature of the oppressions and experiences we face as women, as queer persons and as First Nations and persons of colour.

Having found a lack of resources in the Ottawa region that speak to us, a decision was made to begin a grassroots organization catering to our realities. In addition to fighting oppression, Agitate members aim to provide a gathering space in which we can share our diverse realities in the spirit of celebration.

To this end, Agitate will work towards the promotion of First Nations women and women of colour artists, musicians and performers, both local and from beyond the Ottawa community. Agitate wishes to increase the accessibility of queer-friendly resources catering to First Nations women and women of colour within the cultural, ethnic, health, and other community based resource centres in the Ottawa-area; especially in areas with large newcomer populations. Agitate understands learning as a continuous and life long process. Part of Agitate's mandate is self-education. In particular (but not limited to), the founding members of Agitate will continue to educate themselves on the issues of transphobia and the continuing racist-colonial legacy aimed against First Nations persons.

Dyke March Toronto, 2008

HAWA MIRE

Displaced

Growing up as an African youth here in Canada, my sexual education was seriously inadequate. First because one of the few places where you can learn anything to do with sexual health is at school, and school systems aren't actually teaching using a process that engages and informs students while respecting their experiences and realities. And second, my reality is that if my needs as a racialized woman are not addressed first, I am not as receptive to sexual health workshops or programs.

The media has taught me that sexual crimes that happen to women of colour are less important than those that happen to white women. We are taught this by the inaccurate reporting of our daily news where colour is the perpetrator and white is the victim. And this is compounded by our school systems, when students are told that they are all to be taught the same curriculum, a curriculum that only represents a small fraction of how the world lives.

Sex has always been a particularly uncomfortable topic for me to talk about, much less write about. I remember spending the bulk of my elementary and high school years not understanding the mechanics of sex. My mother gave me a very brief introduction to my menstrual cycle when I was 10 years old, five years before I was to even get my period. My older sisters were having the talk and I was just along for the ride. Sex was considered a taboo topic, not just within my immediate family but my extended family as well.

It's important to understand as well that this notion of uncleanness and sex came about because of colonization, and now exists as a cultural norm. This eradication of historical culture eliminates my parent's ability to teach sex to their children the way their grandparents were taught. My cousins and I would have hushed conversations about how they had their clitoris cut off at the age of four and five when they were living in Kenya and about their theories why it was done. I never understood the extent of what they were talking about until just recently having never been taught anything about Female Genital Mutilation. Once my aunt walked in while we were having one of our conversations and I will never forget the look of disbelief and anger on her face that as girls we were talking about something she considered unclean.

At the age of 21, my sex education has been severely limited and I only realize now how much *not* talking about sexual health has diminished my personal growth and self esteem. School has failed in teaching us anything more than an extended version of the reproductive system in biology classes. This poses a very real problem especially when you take into consideration that if sex education isn't coming from the family and resources are inaccessible, what other options are there for youth?

As for me, I'm now learning things that I wish I had known at 12 or 13; it could have changed the way I look at myself today.

* * *

Hawa Mire *lives in Vancouver, BC and is the co-founder of Point Youth Media, a grassroots organization changing the way youth are viewed through the use of art. Hawa enjoys conversation of all kinds, headbands and large earrings. She is also a strong advocate for the rights of racialized youth, particularly girls.*

WHAT HAPPENS WHEN I SPREAD MY LEGS?

A performed ethnography

by NIDHI PUNYARTHI

When I spread my legs, you see me, woman, brown, cunt, backward, bitchy. You trail your gaze over my hard, diseased body and think of what I hide inside. You think of how easy it is to keep me there, sobbing and quivering at your tip, because there is too much that I hide, too much that I never tell anyone, too much that I keep to myself so that I can explore and become your cunt again.

When I spread my legs, I watch my life flowing, in many different rivers, confounding and diverging along my skin. I release a drenched planet, in which my glistening fingers find their own space to control my sexual health and fertility.

When I spread my legs, I envelope a white woman and let her penetrate. She becomes me, my disease, my glistening life force that makes you blind. And while you grope in the darkness, you miss seeing our brown and pink nipples hardening upon each other and wrestling for the same space.

Worlds of Womaness — *Jennifer Yee*

ESTEFANIA RAMIREZ-TELLO

Culture, Education and Sex

Growing up in an environment culturally hostile towards anything with legs and breasts is not an easy task at all. Especially in a country like Mexico where a man yelling out sexually harassing comments toward any woman crossing by his side of the street is an absolutely normal occurrence. In such places women are expected to grow thick skins and deaf ears at a very early age or risk the public embarrassment of walking through the streets with blood-shot eyes. That's why my mother, bless her soul, pulled me aside at age six to explain the technicalities of human reproduction. Unfortunately for her, her efforts fell on disgusted deaf ears, but my mother, being the unwavering woman she is, proceeded by attempting to give me "the talk" every year ever since. At least until the day she realized that my high school gym teacher had done a better job at "educating" us on sex than she could ever do.

But for a pre-teen girl growing up, accepting her own body and its natural changes is not an easy thing to do at all. And it is complicated even further when that girl knows that the word "development" will be helplessly accompanied with words like "harassment" and the danger of "rape". It is here, in fact, when something as natural as getting your first period becomes nothing short of the date the guillotine will cut mercilessly through your throat.

Perhaps that is why even though I was so terrified of moving to Canada, I was very pleasantly surprised to find no men at any corner ready to throw dirty comments at a ten year old girl. My first actual sexual education class was here in Canada in grade five: however, I recall it as being more of a very mild co-ed introduction on where we may be finding hair growing in our bodies than anything else. By grade six they upgraded to a movie that illustrated the very biological basis of reproduction — but even for that, piles of permission forms were sent weeks in advance to inform frantic parents of what their children would be learning.

In grade seven and eight we progressed from one co-ed sexual education class a year to actual gender segregated classes. But even with the privacy and comfort of a girls-only class deep silence ruled the questions segment. Suddenly I found myself becoming the sex guru among my mostly Chinese and Muslim friends who did not want to ask the teacher questions. And for the first time I realized that the information I took for granted at home was not very well known amongst girls my age of different backgrounds. At that time, my mom volunteered at the information clinic of the Toronto Western Hospital and once I told her the general embarrassment that ruled over the topic she showed me a sexual education pamphlet geared toward teenagers which she'd found at the hospital. Since it was just what we needed my mom took the material to the school, which later ordered more from the hospital and distributed it to us.

However, my most memorable elementary sex-ed talk had to be in grade eight, when our male gym teacher was forced to give a group of nervous teenage girls the sexual education talk because our female gym teacher was ironically on maternity leave. Although a nice enough guy who meant well, the silence in the room could be cut with a knife and the only thing he could do was encourage us to ask him questions about our bodies since he knew more about the topic than we did.

But at last, my most educative, impacting, and final sexual education class came in grade nine. It took up a whole month of the curriculum and this time it was all mandatory. Our female gym-teacher, Heather, had a no-BS approach to sex-ed and had no moral qualms about showing us graphic pictures of every

STD she could get her hands on and every graphic reproduction video she could squeeze in. That highly informative and forever traumatizing month culminated with group projects on our favourite contraceptive method and a final video on child-bearing that had us all swearing off pregnancy for as long as it took for the image to disappear from our minds (which in some cases lasted more than for others). But most importantly, she had us spitting out every contraceptive method in the world and engraved into our minds how to properly use a condom.

Because I did not take gym after grade nine I did not have another sex-ed class until the reproduction segment of grade twelve biology. But nevertheless I will never stop being thankful to both my mother and to Heather for the duty they served in informing girls about the one issue that every girl should be an expert on: her own body and how to protect herself.

* * *

Estefania Ramirez-Tello *is 19-year-old student at York University in Toronto.*

Black Queer Youth Initiative (BQY)

VIJAY SARAVANAMUTHU

Coming Out

I can still remember sitting nervously in one of those little metal chairs with the flip-front desk pads. The air smelled of chalk and Windex and you could count on one fluorescent light to start flickering at any given time.

But what I remember more vividly is the sense of dread I felt every morning of second semester in grade nine. To be more specific; periods two and three — gym class. Although I was never very into team sports or track and field, my anxiety stemmed from the fact that gym class was the one place where I had to face the reality that I was a boy but not quite like the others. In a room where terms like "fag" and "chichi" were part of the daily vernacular, high school gym class was anything but a safe space for me.

But the health units, the two weeks out of the year in which twenty teenage boys with endless supplies of testosterone were crowded into a classroom to talk about sexual health — that was the worst. My own discomfort with my changing body, inability to connect socially with other boys my age and my increasing awareness of my own queer sexuality was only reinforced by sex ed class. I could hear the other boys whispering about me when the teacher started talking about "intercourse." Although the teacher tried to keep the rowdy bunch of us under control, it just wasn't happening. "Vijay never has to worry about getting girls pregnant" I heard them say. And as much as I hated the homophobic environment that I was subject to every morning, they were right. I don't ever have to worry about getting anyone pregnant. The fact of the matter is, the sexual health education that we learned in high school was not designed for me. It was only for my heterosexual counterparts.

Years later, looking back at the traumatic nuances of my high school days I see things quite differently. I can identify a few things that were problematic for me. First of all, the sexual health education curriculum was based on colonially-derived values that only saw sex in a male-female binary dynamic. Heteronormative values also reinforced the homophobic climate that was already making it difficult for me to advocate for my own sexual rights. But my biggest barrier to successfully receiving information about sexual health, HIV and queer issues was the lack of queer-positive support.

Today I work for the Alliance for South Asian AIDS Prevention. My job is to coordinate HIV Prevention programming for gay and bisexual men. I use my lived-experiences to enrich the programming ASAAP provides to youth in high schools. We provide anti-homophobia workshops to classes of grade nine and ten students. Although the primary goal is to educate students on how to protect themselves from HIV and other STIs, we use these platforms to educate youth about cultural and sexual diversity and how this can affect someone's sexual well-being. We deconstruct colonially prescribed identities of "man" and "woman" and look at how word such as "fag" and "dyke" can have an impact on LGBT peoples. As an educator, I feel a sense on accomplishment when I see young minds take a step back to think about how both actions and words can have a profound impact on someone's health. As a queer youth of colour myself, I feel a sense of hope that future generations of queer youth will see workers like myself in high schools and know that they have resources and allies to engage with.

* * *

Vijay Saravanamuthu is an Outreach Coordinator for the Alliance for South Asian AIDS Prevention (ASAAP). ASAAP is a community-based, non-profit, charitable organization committed to providing health promotion, support, education and advocacy in a non-discriminatory manner for those who identify as South Asian living with and affected by HIV/AIDS.

ASAAP conducts outreach at diverse events in and around the City of Toronto. We also have free materials on HIV prevention in Hindi, Urdu, Tamil, Punjabi, Bengali and Gujarati.

ASAAP holds support groups for South Asian Gay, Bisexual and other Men who have Sex with Men (MSM) called Dosti as well as Snehithan which is a group for Tamil Gay, Bisexual, MSM, and Trans people.

ASAAP is also here to offer support on safer sex and related issues so call us!

TONYA KENT

Sexual Assault and Sexual Education — Decolonizing the Solutions

During my university career, I worked on the Sexual Assault Survivors' Support Line (SASSL) at York University in Toronto, Ontario, Canada for four and a half years. Our organization received crisis calls from survivors of sexual assault, trained volunteers to do the same, gave resources for help, and did outreach sessions talking about healthy relationships and sexual assault. SASSL is a pro-feminist, pro-choice, and anti oppressive student run organization.

I volunteered from 2003-2005 and was the coordinator for outreach and resources from 2005-2007. The outreach mostly consisted of outreach about sexual assault and healthy relationships to youth at high schools in the surrounding area of the Jane-Finch community and York University. Jane-Finch is an area of Toronto plagued by drug and gang violence. It mainly consists of youth of colour, mainly of the black community. As the coordinator, it was my responsibility to contact schools about having us come to educate their students on sexual assault and healthy relationships. As an organization that spoke about such a taboo topic, I sometimes had trouble getting into schools. There were a few schools that had young progressive teachers who loved that we wanted to come in. Others that questioned what we wanted to talk about, why we wanted to talk about sexual assault with students, or why we wanted to talk about sexual assault with their male students. Getting into Catholic schools was an even harder feat, as we were questioned about every aspect of our presentation, and forbidden from discussing abortion, birth control of any form, pre-marital sex, and same sex relationships. As you can imagine, those restrictions would make it extremely difficult to talk about healthy relationships and choices after an assault.

Many schools simply didn't want us to come in or apparently couldn't find the time to fit in "that topic". As if sexual assault and healthy relationships aren't important topics for our youth to be knowledgeable about. As well, middle schools for students aged eleven to thirteen NEVER allowed us in, so we had to wait until students reached high school to educate our youth about sexual assault and healthy relationships. When teachers treat sexual assault as if it's a taboo, dirty topic, it makes students also view it that way and less open to discussing it frankly. As well, the delay and secretiveness around such topics allows students to be exposed to and believe sexist and oppressive ideals about relationships and sexual assault.

I've also had the experience of educating drastically different communities; for example, around Jane-Finch, classrooms mostly consisted of black or a diverse range of South Asian students: closer to Bayview largely consisted of white or Asian students of middle to upper class. Sexual education surrounding same sex relationships was seen as disgusting and outside of the norm by students of the Jane-Finch area. Teachers in these classrooms seemed to do nothing to change this belief except to tell me that "those" kids are taught to be that way at home and it's just "their culture". Can you imagine telling me — a black female — that other black students are just "raised that way"? Assuming that this was true, why not try to change such ideals, instead of just accepting them, othering students who view same-sex relationships in a negative way. These students were seen as "unfixable" and the mainly white teachers seemed content to allow students to maintain their negative belief.

In mainly white classrooms, educating students about sexual assault and drugs or alcohol was extremely difficult, especially because those students seemed to feel that if the victim was under the influence of drugs or alcohol, it would not be legally considered a sexual assault. But when students questioned a person's credibility and actions — specifically the female's actions — when it came to sexual assault, teachers were more apt to correct white students on ideas that were oppressive or at least tell them to hear us out. However, with students of colour, teachers seemed to just accept those oppressive ideas and do nothing to change them or at least open their minds to a different idea.

When it comes to understanding sexual assault and the different situations where it happens, in classrooms both of colour and mainly white classrooms, the idea that people "put themselves into those situations" is rampant. The *reactions* towards that idea just seem to be different. In classrooms of colour, often black students expect me to "understand where they're coming from" because I too am a black female and should know that you "just don't go up to someone's hotel room and expect not to have sex". I even had a student tell me once that even though I am teaching about sexual assault, I must not believe those things because "we" weren't raised that way. I thought about this and about being raised in a Caribbean household and realized that even though I believe in pro-feminist and anti-oppressive ideals, I really *wasn't* raised that way. My parents who were born in Trinidad, but immigrated to Canada as adults do not believe in half the things that I protest or advocate for, but yet, I do. I wonder then, how is it that, raised in a household that did not teach me anti-oppressive ideals or pro-feminist beliefs, did I come to understand and believe in those things? EDUCATION. I learned outside of my home certain things and brought them home to my parents who are now getting better at understanding what I believe.

When I say education, I am not necessarily talking about schools. We learned about fallopian tubes, urethras, and ovaries. I think apparently "real" sex education occurred in the twelfth grade when we got to put a condom on a wooden penis. We never talked about sexual feelings and different sexual situations at all. I realize in my time educating that that hasn't changed, as when I start to talk about men and women climaxing, students snicker and giggle and have a hard time believing or understanding how someone can climax or feel good and still be assaulted. The mainstream sex education chooses to treat sex as a legal contract between two people without discussion, about feelings or reactions to sexual activity. I've also seen our mainstream education dirty sex to the point that it is now seen as something dirty by various communities and those views are accepted as such by our educators.

Many times as a coordinator I also encountered teachers who didn't seems to understand why we also wanted to talk to their male students about healthy relationships and sexual assault. This sexist attitude reinforces the belief that only females are responsible for safe sex or anything related to a relationship with "the other". As a coordinator, I was told that the males didn't need that education and I should talk with the female physical education teacher about "that". In my experience though, we did have some teachers that allowed us to talk to their male students, but they were few and far between. When we talked about sexual assault with male students, for example about "No means no" or asking about someone's comfort level or situations of assault, we had teachers questioning what assault was and questioning a survivor's previous actions before the assault.

How can students even learn from us when we're challenged every two seconds with oppressive notions surrounding sexual assault and healthy relationships?

If teachers are expressing oppressive ideals, how are students to be expected not to do the same? How can students even learn from us when we're challenged every two seconds with oppressive notions surrounding sexual assault and healthy relationships? How can students understand that marital rape IS rape when teachers are at the back of the classroom shaking their heads and scoffing? How can students understand that a woman can dress any way she chooses and has the right not to be assaulted when teachers blatantly question that right in front of their students? In a classroom of male students and two female educators of colour, how is it possible for me to get through to students when the white male teacher is questioning our credentials or experience and continually focusing on "those girls that lie about assault"? If the focus is always going to be on the small percentage of people who lie about assault for one reason or another, how can we focus on respecting people's boundaries or how to resolve a conflict in a relationship in a healthy manner?

Educating students in Catholic schools was an even bigger challenge with forbidden topics like same sex relationships, abortion, birth control, and pre-marital sex. How do those students who are in same sex relationships feel when their relationships are treated as something dirty or outside of the norm? How can we discuss safe sex in a healthy relationship if pre-marital sex is not even to be whispered about? How can we discuss choice after an assault if the morning after pill or abortion is a forbidden topic because we're in a Catholic school? How did we get to the point that we decided that educating our youth on premarital sex was wrong? Who decided that marriage was the indicator of whether sex was right or wrong? What about students of different communities who are taught differently? I know that as a black female, my community wasn't the one who decided that any discussion around sex was dirty and taboo.

It is impossible to have a full discussion about healthy relationships if important aspects of that discussion are ignored or treated as taboo. We can't discuss a healthy sexual relationship if a relationship outside of marriage is not treated as a real relationship. We can't discuss sexual assault fully if we only view it as a stereotypical occurrence when a strange man jumps out of a bush and assaults a young attractive woman. If we don't recognize that sexual assault is something that happens in same sex relationships, marital relationships, long and short term relationships, and acquaintance relationships, we can't have a proper discussion nor can our youth be educated properly.

This sounds as though I've never had a good experience as a sexual assault/healthy relationships educator, but I have. I've had students change their minds, I've seen students challenge other students' oppressive ideals, I've had teachers be extremely grateful to us for coming in and invited us back, I've had students who ask me about getting involved in sexual education after our presentations, and all these things have made me happy and glad to have been an educator, but these happy instances happen less often than the unhappy instances.

In my opinion, if we want to educate our youth about healthy relationships and sexual assault, our educators first need to be educated. We can't have oppressive teachers spreading oppressive ideas to impressionable youth. As a society, we need to accept other peoples' choices in partners and treat those choices and relationships the same way we treat heterosexual relationships and educate our youth to do so as well. We also have to stop viewing sex as dirty and stop viewing sexual education as something that corrupts youth to "go out and do it". Sexual assault is a huge issue in our society and if our youth, male and female, are educated properly, they can truly understand the impact that sexual assault has on a person and not view assault with oppressive ideals.

We also need to take into account that our youth in Canada come from very diverse communities and we need to educate in a non-oppressive manner that doesn't assume that our youth need only to learn the colonizer's belief surrounding sex and healthy relationships. We need to stop viewing sexual assault in a sexist way that always blames that survivor. I honestly don't have a solution to all the questions that I posed, nor do I have an answer to HOW we can stop oppressive ideas surrounding healthy relationships and sexual assault other than, EDUCATION. Educating our youth is the best and only way to keep them smart and safe and when everyone understands that, we can begin to REALLY educate our youth.

* * *

__Tonya Kent__ is a black young female who was previously a Sexual Assault/Healthy Relationships Educator at York University. She is originally from Toronto, but is currently residing in Santiago, Dominican Republic where she teaches English.

The Canadian Artists Against Sexual Assault (CAASA) began on December 22nd, 2006 with a central goal to generate more awareness of the prevalence of sexual assault in Canada by using art as a communication and educational tool. Online web portal, Facebook.com was the starting point for the group. Here, CAASA Director, Bryn Ludlow launched the group and began inviting friends and colleagues to join. Many are former schoolmates and have built the foundation of CAASA as Directors and Program leaders with backgrounds in Women's Studies, Business, Design and Communications, Media and Public Relations, Psychology, Sociology and Political Sciences. Since then over ninety members have joined, and membership is open to all visitors to the site.

We operate as an online group and all members participate in discussion topics about sexual assault and violence issues. We plan to have annual art auctions, concerts and performances by CAASA members and external artists to support local and regional Rape Crisis centres and Victim Services Programs in Canada.

"Perseverance is more prevailing than violence; and many things

which cannot be overcome when they are together, yield themselves

up when taken little by little."

— Plutarch

CAASA
Canadian Artists Against Sexual Assault
Artistes Canadiens Contre L'Assaut Sexuel
ACCAS

Sexual Assault & Domestic Violence Resources in Toronto

Disclaimer:
CAASA/ACCAS is not responsible for the content/information in the web links or articles. Some of the material may be upsetting/triggering to individuals. We have chosen the resources based on a peer review of the services offered by each organization and have tried to include a diverse array of services in Toronto.

† Service Availble en français
This document is available for download: www.igloo.org/caasaweb

Toronto Crisis Centres

The Toronto Rape Crisis Centre/ Multicultural Women Against Rape †
17 Phoebe Street, Toronto, Ontario
24 hour Crisis Line: (416) 597-1171
info@trccmwar.ca
http://www.trccmwar.ca/
crisis@trccmwar.ca

Assaulted Women's Helpline †
http://www.awhl.org/
24 hour Crisis Line: (416) 863-0511

Elle-ecoute (Crisis hotline for French-speaking women) †
GTA: (416) 657-2229
Toll-Free: 1 (877) 679-2229
http://www.oasisfemmes.com/

Peel Region Sexual Assault/Domestic Violence Program †
(905) 571-3344 x116
http://www.satcontario.com/Network/centres.shtml

Victim Services Toronto †
40 College Street
Toronto, Ontario M5G 2J3
(416) 808-7066
http://www.victimservicestoronto.com

Telehealth Ontario/ Télésanté Ontario Free Access to a Registered Nurse — 24 Hours a day, 7 days a Week. †
1-866-797-0000
TTY : 1-866-797-0007

Legal Guidance and Court Preparation Services

Legal Aid Ontario †
http://www.legalaid.on.ca/

The Barbra Schlifer Clinic †
(416) 323-9149
489 College Street, Toronto, Ontario
http://www.schliferclinic.com

Sexual Assault Survivors Information on Canadian Law on Sexual Assault
sexualassault@aloak.ca
http://sexualassault.aloak.ca/

Ministry of the Attorney General Ontario Victim Services Secretariat Victim/Witness Assistance Program †
18 King Street East, 7th Floor
Toronto, Ontario, M5C 1C4
Victim Support Line, (416) 314–2447 in Toronto, or toll free at 1 (888) 579–2888.
http://www.attorneygeneral.jus.gov.on.ca

Emergency Medical Care & Specialized Programs

CWHN: Getting Through Medical Examinations. A Resource for Women Survivors of Abuse and Their Health Care Providers
http://www.cwhn.ca/resources/csa/index.php

Women's College Hospital †
76 Grenville Street, Toronto, Ontario
- Sexual Assault & Domestic Violence Care Centre, 1st Floor; (416) 323-6040
- Trauma Therapy Program (TTP) 9th Floor; (416) 323-6400 ext. 4230 ttp@wchospital.ca
- Women Recovering from Abuse Program (WRAP) 9th Floor0 (416) 323-6400, ext. 4863 wrap@wchospital.ca

Sexual Assault Care Centre
The Scarborough Hospital. Grace Div.†
3030 Birchmount Road
Scarborough, Ontario
(416) 495-2555
http://www.sacc.to

Child & Youth Sexual Assault & Domestic Violence Programs

Kids Help Phone †
1 (800) 668-6868
http://www.kidshelpphone.ca/

Kite Project: Support groups for children who have witnessed violence
(416) 636-9963

SCAN project: child abuse counseling for children
(416) 598-6275

THE HINCKS-DELLCREST TREATMENT CENTRE †
Jarvis Street Site
440 Jarvis Street Toronto, Ontario,
Canada M4Y 2H4
(416) 924-1164

BOOST: Child Abuse Prevention & Intervention †
890 Yonge St., 11th Floor
Toronto, Ontario M4W 3P4
Tel: (416) 515-1100 Fax: (416) 515-1227

LGBTQ Sexual Assault & Domestic Violence Servies

519 Community Centre †
519 Church Street, Toronto, Ontario, M4Y 2C9, Phone: 416-392-6874
http://www.the519.org/
- Community Counselling Program 416-392-6874 x 335
- The 519 Anti-Violence Programme avp@the519.org
- Reporting LGBT bashing 416-392-6878 Ex. 337

Lesbian Gay Bi Youth Line Youth peer support and counselling †
1-800-268-9688
416-962-9688
www.youthline.ca

SAFE: Stop Abuse For Everyone †
16869 SW 65th Ave PMB 212
Lake Oswego, OR 97035-7865 U.S.A.
(503) 853-8686; http://www.safe4all.org

Services for Male Survivors of Sexual Assault and Domestic Violence

Male Survivor
(613) 230-6179
180 Argyle Avenue, Suite 321
Ottawa, Ontario, Canada
general@malesurvivor.ca
http://www.malesurvivor.ca/

SAVIS: Sexual Assault and Violence Intervention Services of Halton
24 hour crisis line: (905) 875-1555
(905) 825-3743 TTY
*If you are Deaf or Hard of Hearing and calling after-hours, please call crisis line using Bell Relay service

The Men's Project †
180 Argyle Avenue, Suite 321
Ottawa, Ontario, Canada
K2P 1B7
Tel: (613) 230-6179
Toll Free for Ontario: 1-877-677-6532
Fax: (613) 230-6173
http://themensproject.ca

The White Ribbon Campaign †
365 Bloor St. East, Toronto, Ontario, Canada M4W 3L4
Phone: (416) 920-6684
Toll Free: 1-800-328-2228
Fax: (416) 920-1678
Email: info@whiteribbon.ca
http://www.whiteribbon.ca

EILEEN SATO

Sexual Attitudes and Japanese Youth

The way that we deal with sexuality as Japanese people is quite conservative in nature. Yet at the same time because of colonization, imperialism, and the World War, we had to change. You could say that we've had a lot of Western influences, and our identity is highly politicized at every angle.

Japan also invaded several places, and forced imperialism the same way Europe did to Aboriginal people here in Canada. Colonized Japanese culture dictates that you have to be more secluded as a person, like the island itself. So similar to a lot of thing that are deemed more personal, like sexuality, people will try and walk around the issue. They know it's there, but they pretend like it's not. This negative attitude towards sex is extremely dangerous, and we know with youth today what kind of negative implications it can cause.

I never talked about sex with my parents. They kind of expected that I would know about it somehow. Sexuality is something that people just don't talk about. It's funny — having been born and living in Canada, I'm so much more exposed to it than if I were to be around my friends from Japan. I have a friend here who is Japanese and interestingly enough, we do talk about it openly. There's a "Canadian" side to us that makes us be more open.

Colonization in Japan happened quite some time ago, but there was major resistance to it. During the 1700's, the Dutch tried to come in and the Emperor simply did not allow it. Then the 1800's came and Japan was in a situation where people were still fighting with swords and thought they needed to modernize more. So the Dutch came in and Westernization started. They brought with them guns, canon balls, etc. In the Edo-period, the whole country was in chaos. The South, the most traditional area where you have Samurai's, was entirely in turmoil and began losing their ancestral means of life. Everyone had a specific way of living, and the traditional way they wanted to live was completely outlawed. The Emperor essentially said "we are going to change how you have been living for thousands and thousands of years, so deal with it". As Westernization continued to come in from Tokyo and other Northern regions, there was a lot of violence and civil wars. This brought in religion as well, and when some people tried to resist it, genocide happened.

During WWII, a lot of Western things were forbidden. People were trying to take everything away and force so-called "patriotism" on people. Religion was kicked out, and people had to go underground. And there were certainly worse things that happened than the bombing in Hiroshima. Okinawa, the southern most islands of Japan, is coincidentally where the United States reserved the best areas, resort wise. When Iwo Jima fell, the first place they attacked was Okinawa, where thousands and thousands of women were brutally raped. A lot of people were forced to be Westernized in their sexuality, and this really all ties in to what's going on now.

Throughout Japanese history, there has constantly been this acceptance that men will always have that need for sex. We do have geishas, but geishas are not sex workers, they are entertainers. Orians are sex workers, and this has been around for a long time. There are also love hotels that charge by the hour, whose sole purpose is for people to have sex in them. It's really male-dominated, and women seem to be silenced with having any say in the matter of pleasure for their own bodies. The traditional side of Japanese culture makes it difficult for them to come to terms with it. For example, even my own parents still think I'm a virgin!

In the 90's, there was a TV show where a young woman involved herself in sex work to get tickets to a concert, and it showed people that yeah, sex is out there. Even a female perspective on the realities of our sexuality was shown! But the fact that she got HIV when she did this just scared people. This is definitely not the most effective way to go about educating people.

Yet today when you go to the "red light" district in Japan, it's all out there. It's a double standard, guys can talk about it, but girls can't. If girls do talk about it, it's frowned upon amongst guys. If there's a girl who's more open with her sexuality, she's automatically seen as promiscuous. If she doesn't talk about sex, she's seen as wife material, with desirable domestic values intact. She's just not supposed to do it.

If there's a girl who's more open with her sexuality, she's automatically seen as promiscuous. If she doesn't talk about sex, she's seen as wife material, with desirable domestic values intact.

I went to a Catholic high school here in Canada, and I had a lot of issues with it. I don't think that religion, sexuality, and your body in general should be all taught in one. Catholicism teaches you about morals and forces you into a cookie-cutter shape that says "oh you are supposed to have a family, save yourself until marriage" and it really doesn't make any sense. Not everyone is going to be that way! We all have different lives. The way we were taught in Catholic school is just not practical. What about healthy relationships? What about things we actually need and can apply? It's quite ridiculous actually how they taught us and thought that it was the right way to do it. I often wonder if public schools might have taught me that there are multiple viewpoints on this very important topic. The one thing all schools lack is incorporating all of who we are.

I think that's why we have all this unhealthiness going on with our youth, it has to do with the fact that we are being taught the wrong way. We were taught that sex is a bad thing. Your peers echo what they get taught, and words like "slut" start going around. We get shunned.

But I was different; I taught myself how to have a healthy sexual relationship. It was trial and error. I wasn't taught what I needed to know, but I survived.

For me, you can look at it in two different angles that are equally confusing to reconcile. On the one hand I feel like I'm

Canadian since I was born here, and on the other hand people don't think I'm Canadian because of how I look; so in reality, how am I to be influenced? What should I follow? It gets to be a very negative state of mind when these kinds of standards are predetermined for me, and stereotypes are so easy to buy into. But I know now that there are different outlets that exist where I can have choice, and decide what's right for me.

For anyone in my generation, born in Canada, we're essentially on our own. In a way, Japanese people have gone through so much colonization, it's like we're ready for the next thing we have to adapt to. And although we'd like to think that it might be the best thing for us, it's really not always and we should challenge that happening to us. Isolation breeds close-mindedness, and it's hard to see where we even began and what's really ours.

Japanese youth need to know about healthy sexual relationships, STI's, and sexuality in general. They need to know that they can make choices, and that they should decide what's best for their own bodies. I wish from a younger age that they wouldn't be so prudish and so shy, that parents would be willing to talk about it, and it always needs to happen a lot sooner than everyone thinks. The fact that the information is not made available means they will go elsewhere, and that might not be so reliable. And I think we can all do a much better job of that.

* * *

Eileen Sato *is a 23-year-old Japanese Canadian who works as a dental hygienist. She is a survivor of the Catholic education system who barely made it. She's currently an atheist, and believes it's important to be who you are and talk about sex when you want!*

ADAM BENN

Moving Beyond Sexual Education

I did not receive sexual education because I am gay. As bold as that statement might be to some, it is very true if you consider that I learned about gay sex through the Grade 8 rumour mill. Learning at 13 that gay men "insert their penis into each other's bums" was the beginning and the end of my gay sexual education in school and the reality is that "gay sex" is a topic that remains taboo within school walls. By refusing to openly teach gay sex as a natural and important component of life, sexual education is failing to educate youth with the understanding that youth are diverse individuals, not a homogenous collective group that can be serviced by one model.

The state of our sexual education in Canada is appalling because it fails to address the multifaceted needs of individual youth. Rather, "sexual education" perpetuates dominant ideologies that are continually used to oppress marginalized communities. In order for sexual health education in Canada to be an effective service, it needs to cater to the individual needs of those who are accessing it. Sexual health providers in education must begin to recognize and acknowledge the diverse backgrounds of the individuals and develop an education system to address that individuality, rather than attempt to force today's youth to adopt a "cookie cutter" sexual health model that is constructed by heterosexual hegemony. By adopting an individualistic, anti-oppressive model, school can reduce the marginalization of many groups, including the LGBTQ2 community.

Throughout school, I had regular education about heterosexual sex. Starting from Grade 2, the TCDSB's "Fully Alive" series began documenting sex as "The Miracle of Life". By the time I reached Grade 8, I had fully been exposed to the wonders of my sexuality, albeit through a Catholic framework. My sexual education in high school was limited to a two-week discussion surrounding STDs and STIs in Grade 10 health. All in all, I would say that my sexual health education would have left me adequately prepared — if I were heterosexual. However, this was a system that failed to consider my individual needs, and left me increasingly vulnerable when I was already "at-risk". Homosexuals are heavily stigmatized in society, which restricts the ability to access information from sources that are often taken for granted, such as parents and the media. Extreme danger arises when one considers how many "at-risk" factors are in play with homosexual youth — the most obvious being the lack of HIV/AIDS education, — which is crucial in a community where HIV rates are the highest. However, issues surrounding depression, mental health and drug use are frequently at play. Through ages 12-18, I was constantly questioning my sexuality and being teased in high school as a result. The fear existed that I would be found out, beat up, or ostracized (which equals social death in high school). The coming out experience was and continues to be a tough battle that I fought alone. And like many other homosexual youth, I struggled and continue to struggle with issues of mental health while forging an identity that goes against my own socialization and is in opposition to societal norms.

My education in gay sexual health came partially from books and the Internet. The Toronto Public library was a great resource, even through my face would burn with shame when I checked out gay sex books. However, a large chunk of it came through a community agency that gave me the tools I need to protect myself. In my senior high school years, I was involved in a LGBTQ group for youth through the East Metro Community Services. This group was not only a great networking space to meet other queer youth as myself, also served as an invaluable resource for extracting the necessary information on proper condom use, protection from STDs/STI, drug use in the gay community and HIV/AIDS, all coming from a non-judgmental, anti-oppressive framework.

As I work within the social services sector, I find myself facing challenges in delivering an effective sexual education model. I must acknowledge that the "sexually liberal" and "sex-positive" framework within which I work has been shaped by my experiences and my identity as a "black gay man". And as a "black gay man" I have my biases and ideas of what sexual education should look like. I also must acknowledge the wide racial and religious diversities of the communities in which I work, and how this diversity impacts ideas of what sexual education should or should not be. Working with Somali, Vietnamese, Bengali, Chinese, Spanish and Black youth often means that one service model does not fit all. Cultural differences regarding sex and education, language barriers and socioeconomic status are all factors that impact the sexual education service model in the social services sector. Similarly, working with strict orthodox Muslim and Christian families poses another challenge as many of the young Muslim girls that I work with come from strict families that discourage premarital sex. These young girls often find it difficult to obtain safe sex knowledge or to safely engage in sexual activities. This makes it difficult to adequately service such a diverse community with strong opinions and divergent ideologies, especially in regards to sexuality.

I also must acknowledge the wide racial and religious diversities of the communities in which I work, and how this diversity impacts ideas of what sexual education should or should not be.

The essential component of delivering an effective sexual education model is through respecting and acknowledging the ethno-cultural and sexual diversity and uniqueness of individuals. Adopting an anti-oppressive and non-judgmental approach means that I must consider the values and beliefs of the individuals that I service, and ensure that I provide information to that individual based on his or her needs. We all have our biases, myself included, but the danger arises when we allow these biases to permeate into our service models and determine what information we share and how we share it. Giving sexual education advice to young Muslim women may go against the values of their families and community; however, in a world where the presence of HIV/AIDS makes sexual education a life or death matter, I will be doing a great disservice to my youth to educate them based on what I think they need to know versus what they actually need to know.

Teaching gay youth about gay sex in schools might offend parents or the church, but the reality is that these individuals need access to this information if they are to be able to protect themselves. An anti-oppressive service model exists within these agencies; we need not reinvent the wheel. However, this non-judgmental framework must be incorporated into the dominant and powerful societal structures such as schools to provide service for individuals as well as challenge the ideologies that enable marginalization of LGBT, racialized and other disadvantaged groups. Eliminating this marginalization is a hefty task, but it starts with examining the prejudices built into the structures and services that currently exist.

* * *

Adam Benn *is a 23-year-old community worker in Regent Park who currently resides in Toronto.*

Toronto District School Board

Human Sexuality Program
Social Work Services, School Services
Anti-Homophobia
Group Work for <u>YOUR</u> Classroom

The TDSB has approved an Equity Policy Statement which requires that ideals related to anti-homophobia and sexual orientation equity be reflected in all aspects of organizational structures, polices, guidelines, procedures, classroom practices, day-to-day operations, and communication practices. (Section 3: Anti-Homophobia, Sexual Orientation and Equity, TDSB Equity Foundation Statement & Commitments to Equity Policy Implementation, pg. 21)

Elementary Panel (grades k-6)
<u>Family Values Workshop</u> - We Value ALL Families...

- definitions (gay, lesbian, straight, homophobia)
- NFB videos (Apples & Oranges, Sticks & Stones) - a discussion of family diversity and the impact of homophobic bullying, name-calling; for grades 1-3: story-telling with video clip from, "That's a Family!"
- exercise, "What's a normal family?" and/or "Same and Different" and/or "Porcupine Game" that explores homophobic name-calling

Middle School

- <u>General discussions</u> of lesbian, gay, bisexual issues that uses the ***porcupine exercise*** *- following some definitions, the exercise explores homophobia, what motivates it and how it impacts on people...* this may also be accompanied with question/answer component where the students hear from a panel of young people who speak of their experience as lesbian, gay and bisexual youth and youth with lesbian, gay and bisexual parents
- <u>Hate Crimes</u> - through the use of video and an interactive exercise ("pyramid of hate"), students are engaged in a discussion that looks at hate crime on a broad level with a specific focus to anti-gay hate crime.... the discussion also focuses on how to fight hate...

Secondary Schools (**the following list is just some of the past types of group work offered**)
(The following topics also include a discussion of definitions of common terms...)

- <u>General Discussion</u> of lesbian, gay and bisexual issues that may use interactive exercises (such as the porcupine game-see above), NFB Video ("In Other Words") - featuring lgbt students, some from the TDSB; possibly a question/answer panels of lesbian, gay and bisexual youth
- <u>Hate Crimes</u> (see above); <u>Legal issues</u> facing lesbian, gay and bisexual persons (generally, and in roles as parents and spouses);
- <u>History</u> (e.g. the origin of the pink and black triangle in Nazi concentration camps);**Family Studies**; <u>Health and Sexuality....</u> (phys.ed and health classes) as it pertains to lesbian, gay and bisexual issues

For more info please contact: Steven Solomon, MSW, RSW
School Social Worker, Human Sexuality Program & Triangle Program, TDSB,
Tel: (416) 985-3749,
Email: steven.solomon@tdsb.on.ca

RE-ACT!

A Project of Youth Action Network and Gendering Adolescent AIDS Prevention

This manual, designed for youth by youth, features a diverse range of projects put forward by passionate, inspiring and fired-up individuals committed to social change. Each individual, group and project are committed to eradicating HIV. This includes challenging stigma, informing the public about the ties between funding and disease, educating other youth on the connection between global and local issues, throwing parties to raise money and awareness, and creating spaces within particular communities to talk about the issues. And ..... each project is accomplished with the help of art! This ain't your stuck-in-a-stuffy-museum art project either. Youth across the city are using the art forms they know best to challenge, educate, and question the presence of the HIV/AIDS epidemic in their local and global communities: hip hop, button making, fashion, visual art, stickering, collage, web design, graphic design .... the list goes on!

What you'll see here:
The next few pages include a small sampling of what's to come! The complete manual will highlight eight features by savvy youth activists, an article on one young woman's journey in taking action, tips and tricks for getting involved, a glossary section and a heavy but light-inspired list of resources.

You'll notice that the focus of each feature is an interview. These interviews were conducted through online communication with each of the featured participants, so that individuals could take as long as they needed to compose their responses. Each participant was sent interview questions (similar to a survey format) with simple instructions:

> *"Use this as your soap box! The questions are purposely broad so that you may have the freedom to answer them, or challenge them, as you see fit".*

Some participants even changed the questions asked! Unlike traditional interviews where the interviewer asks all the questions and waits patiently for a response, I wanted this process to be as open and equitable as possible. I hoped that by providing space and time, it might counteract the challenges that some youth may face by having to write responses.

The finished manual will be done in the winter of 2009 and can be found online at www.youthactionnetwork.org. While we don't know the exact url just yet, please check out the site — and search for the link!

Why youth?

The 2007 UN Epi Report categorizes HIV prevalence rates in two categories: adult and children. They define children as 15 years and under. Does this mean adults count as anyone who is aged 16 years and up?! What about youth? While the definition for youth varies, in a Canadian context, youth are generally regarded as being between the age of 16-24, however this range can begin as low as 12 and range to 29. When discussing sexual and reproductive health, and HIV/AIDS youth face particular challenges that are different from the challenges experienced by "adults". This extends beyond sexuality and connects to larger issues such as housing, schooling and employment. Youth need spaces and platforms to speak to important issues affecting their sexual and reproductive health. This is on account of age, but is linked with other social markers such as gender, race, class, sexual orientation, ability, geographical location (i.e rural youth vs. urban youth), place of birth, and citizenship status. When we talk about "youth" and HIV/AIDS, we must recognize that "youth" make up an incredibly diverse community, even in Toronto.

These challenges equate to real numbers.

Globally, while reported HIV rates among youth are low, they are quickly rising, particularly among young women. For example, in Canada (2006), females accounted for 40.9% of positive HIV test reports among youth aged 15 to 29 years.

There has also been a recent increase in sexually transmitted infection (STI) rates among youth (Public Health Agency of Canada). But what does this have to do with HIV?! An increase in undetected STIs increases an individual's biological risk of contracting HIV. This may also indicate social risks, such as access to sexual health clinics, and the ability to negotiate condom use in relationships. Furthermore, the Canadian AIDS Society states that "Because young people with HIV progress to AIDS much more slowly than older persons, AIDS statistics are bound to disproportionately under-represent youth" (Canadian AIDS Society, 2003). And education is lagging far behind! The Toronto Teen Survey, facilitated by GAAP and Planned Parenthood has discovered that only 62% of youth are receiving sexual health education in schools. Other youth report receiving sexual health education in youth or religious groups. But, 10% of all youth surveyed reported that they have never received any sexual health education! Woah!!

We need equitable sex education which speaks to all youth —not by homogenizing sex ed, but by recognizing that different people and communities have different needs. This ain't math class where there's only one formula, or one correct answer. By silencing honest, open discussion about HIV/AIDS, we do ourselves and our communities a giant injustice. I hope that this manual may provide a platform for youth to speak to important issues not only within the confines of these pages, but outside of these pages in classrooms, cafeterias, on the streets and in bedrooms across the city.

Just think about what we could accomplish! According to the UN World Youth Report (2003), young people make up almost a fifth of the world's population. As youth, it's important that we speak out, talk to our friends, and family members about the importance of HIV/AIDS, not just as something which happens "over there" but something which happens here, in our very own backyards.

Youth of colour and HIV/AIDS

Each of the youth featured in the next few pages are youth of colour. Youth of colour face particular challenges when dealing with mainstream sexual health and HIV/AIDS programming. This is particularly problematic given the increased risk of HIV for particular communities; social economic factors such as systems of oppression (sexism, racism, homophobia, etc), poverty, migration, and stigma increase the risk of contracting HIV. These are sometimes called "social determinants of health".

However, being from a community where HIV is or is not prevalent does not make someone any more or less accountable for the epidemic. As local and global citizens, we all have a role to play in both the spread and reduction of HIV/AIDS. Our actions have consequences both positive and negative. So step it up! Talk to your friends, family and community about HIV/AIDS, and what it means to be both community member, and ally.

How to use this guide

Fired up but don't know what to do? Have inspiration but no means of action?

This guide is designed for individuals and activists who are interested in activating their knowledge, passion and skills and want to fuel these ideas into positive action. More specifically, the following pages focus on using the arts as a catalyst or medium for HIV/AIDS youth activism. By focusing on a broad range of arts-based education and activist efforts organized by committed youth, this guide aims to inspire action, provoke bursts of insight, and begin a (soon-to-be-digital) dialogue between and among HIV/AIDS youth activists across the city. There are already an abundance of general resources for youth activism circulating in local libraries, schools, community centres and youth organizations. This guide tries to specifically map out some of the successes and challenges encountered by young HIV/AIDS arts activists. Stop looking 'out there' and start looking 'in here': there's already a wealth of knowledge in our communities.

Enjoy!

Sarah Switzer
Writer and Coordinator, HIV/AIDS Youth Arts Activism Manual

* * *

Gendering Adolescent AIDS Prevention (GAAP) *is a team of researchers (faculty and graduate students) working in several research sites and interested in participatory approaches to working with young people in relation to sexuality, HIV prevention and AIDS awareness. In our work we have a number of projects and research studies. The overall goal of this work is to develop gender-based analyses of HIV/AIDS that can be used in prevention programs with youth.*

Youth Action Network (YAN) *is dedicated to helping youth become more informed and actively involved in order to move towards a just and sustainable society. We strongly believe in the ability of youth to affect change in the world. We understand the need for a stronger voice and for greater participation in our local and global communities. The main functions of YAN are to provide information and promote action. YAN is a national non-profit youth organization based in Toronto.*

Respect to the Real Writa – Anonymous Artist in Montreal

RE-ACT!

Nidhi Punyarthi

Youth Action Network
Gendering Adolescent AIDS Prevention Project

I met Nidhi four years ago when I first became involved with HIV/AIDS work. Nidhi was involved with so many fascinating projects. I would see photographs Nidhi took in a Photovoice project mounted at our school, and exhibited all over the city. I finally met Nidhi in my third year of university at the University of Toronto, where we were learning how to create performed ethnography on HIV/AIDS. Performed ethnography is a way of representing research through performance. With a group of other students, we worked together to analyze data and turn it into monologues and short plays. Later, I had the pleasure of performing these monologues and plays with Nidhi at local, regional and even national conferences! Nidhi always stole the show — her passion, creativity, intensity, and strong ability to articulate herself both through art, and in conversation always wowed me.

...she still continues to impress me to this day.

Project Description:

PhotoVoice: This workshop was a follow up to a presentation on the structural determinants of HIV risk from a gender and global perspective. Participants were members of the New College, Youth Advisory Board for the Gendering Adolescent AIDS Prevention (GAAP) Project, University of Toronto. Youth were given disposable cameras and asked to work in small groups to take photographs that reflected ideas and/or issues about gender and HIV/AIDS raised in the presentation. When the photos were developed, each group was asked to write about their images using the following questions as a guide: 1) What is happening in this photo? 2) Why did you take this photo? 3) How does this photo relate to gender and HIV/AIDS 4) What is a good caption for your photo? All photos were then displayed on a large blank mural with room for all workshop participants to comment on the images produced by other groups. Since the workshop, many of these photographs have been used to develop a youth media toolkit for HIV/AIDS education.

> *"Youth media can be a powerful avenue for allowing young people the opportunity to develop their own messages and representations of issues like HIV/AIDS. TIGXpress- HIV/AIDS centres on global education as a tool for change with Photovoice and the internet as instruments for creating new forms of transnational dialogue. In a world increasingly devastated by AIDS, building solidarities and alliances among youth may be the best hope for curbing the disease. Photography may provide a universal language for communicating about AIDS and for opening new avenues for youth global activism".*
>
> *— The TIGXpress - HIV/AIDS toolkit*

Interview Questions

NAME: Nidhi Punyarthi
AGE: 22
LOCATION: Toronto/Ottawa

How did you get started? What led you to pursue HIV/AIDS activism?
I attended a workshop where students engaged in creative projects to communicate knowledge and ideas about HIV/AIDS. I found this to be a very useful and important process, as much literature on HIV/AIDS that I had come across earlier did not address the knowledge and concerns of disadvantaged groups. This realization inspired me to participate in activities of the Gendering Adolescent AIDS Prevention Project, where I evaluated educational materials, used theatre as a means of communicating missing or silenced discourses on HIV/AIDS, and started some of my own projects on cross-cultural translation of HIV/AIDS experiences.

What about your project got you fired up?
My project was inspired after I attended the International AIDS 2006 Conference in Toronto. I met activists from different countries and who

spoke different languages. A lot of people expressed to me a realization that Toronto was not what they expected — and that the so-called international conference had a very specific linguistic (English) and cultural (Canadian-hegemonic) focus. I had also been involved with the Francophone Centre of Toronto, who had a booth at the Conference and took the reins in accommodating for the shortcomings of the larger international conference. A lot of different grassroots groups at the conference tried to do just that.

As a French speaker and a student in Toronto who participated in both GAAP and the Francophone Centre activities (http://www.centrefranco.org/), I thought of combining the two under "francophone projects". This turned out to be a very fruitful venture because it started dialogue between university students and community members on issues that touched racial and linguistic minorities in Toronto (such as Black francophones), which were never the focus of discussion topics in larger conferences. Non-English speaking immigrant populations in Toronto are at a crisis for not receiving accessible and adequate health and information services.

Why do you do this work?
I am passionate about increasing the accessibility of services and information, in the most general and encompassing sense.

Why art?
Art is a medium that is flexible, plural, diverse and fairly accessible. Using dramatic arts to speak to, speak from, and speak with different experiences has been a very productive method of knowledge creation for myself and my peers.

Do you have any suggestions or tips for youth who are interested in pursuing or already working on HIV/AIDS arts activism models?
I suggest keeping an open mind. Sometimes, when you are engrossed and passionate in your cause, you can tend to overlook other related and sometimes conflicting causes, even though you think you are open-minded. It is important to see power emanating from yourself as well. Power is always a multi-way street. Ask yourself what impact you have on yourself and others when you do your work. That is one way to be mindful of your actions and to keep flexible in your activism.

* * *

BIO

Nidhi is a 23 year old woman, completing her Bachelor of Law at the University of Ottawa. During her involvement at Gendering Adolescent AIDS Prevention, she wrote for the magazine of the Youth Action Network and was involved in focus groups on youth perceptions of HIV/AIDS and sexuality. She also participated in a PhotoVoice workshop that led to the creation of an HIV/AIDS educational guide. She has also written a performed ethnography that challenges dominant notions of South Asian womens' sexuality, and has presented it at various conferences. More recently, she worked on a collaborative and bilingual (French-English) performed ethnography project with the Francophone Centre of Toronto. Nidhi is now establishing herself in Ottawa and exploring the field of environmental justice.

Participants: 10
Time commitment/week: 3 hours every two weeks
For how long?: Meeting biweekly over 2 Months
Space required: A board room in the university

Photovoice participants were asked to discuss each of the photos using the following questions, as guides. What do you think these photos mean? Look at each photo, and ask yourself or your friends the following:

- What do we SEE in this photograph?
- What is really HAPPENING? What does the photo represent?
- How is this connected to HIV/AIDS?
- How does this story relate to OUR lives?
- Why does this problem or strength exist? What are the root causes?
- How might we become EMPOWERED now that we better understand the problem?
- What can we DO about it?

"One Size Fits All?

"Hey, your health's for sale!"

A young South Asian woman is researching immigration laws on a Canadian website. The highlighted text emphasizes the discriminatory language and practices of Canadian immigration policies. The woman's position and the angled profile of her mouth and hands communicate her despair. International regulation takes place around HIV/AIDS, and borders "tighten and whiten" against HIV/AIDS-affected migrants

To See More Photos Online:
http://www.takingitglobal.org/express/gallery/artwork/collections.html?type=tig&collectionID=839

Some Definitions

Discourse = This word can be used in many different ways. However, here discourse is used to refer to the type of language used to discuss a particular issue. Pay attention to how language can affect the interpretation of HIV/AIDS by society. The way HIV/AIDS is discussed and described can have a very powerful impact in shaping, often false, beliefs about the illness.

Gender inequality = Although it can impact males as well, gender inequality commonly refers to the devaluing of females and imposing on them barriers to person freedom, education, jobs or equal pay, legal rights and/or political representation. It is linked to HIV/AIDS as such inequality places women in more vulnerable situations and at greater risk for contracting HIV. For example, women in many countries often lack access to education and opportunities for employment. Therefore they easily become dependant on their husbands for economic support. Their dependency makes them vulnerable to the sexual requests of their male partner. They cannot refuse sexual requests for fear of being thrown out of the relationship. Women may endure sexual abuse, unwanted unprotected sex or have an unfaithful partner, all increasing their risk of contracting HIV/AIDS.

Transnational dialogue = Engaging in communication and discussion across national boundaries. Transnational dialogue presents enormous opportunities for learning and communicating knowledge about HIV/AIDS.

Solidarity = Solidarity refers to the ties that bind social groups together. Often, social groups come together for a common cause, for example, people from around the world are coming together in fighting to stop the spread of the HIV/AIDS pandemic. However, solidarity doesn't always mean that everyone within a group thinks the same. Solidarity can allow for difference among unified groups.

For more info on HIV/AIDS and South Asian Communities:
The Alliance for South Asian AIDS Prevention
www.asaap.ca

Alliance for South Asian AIDS Prevention – Brown Kiss Youth Site
http://www.brownkiss.ca/

Asian Community AIDS Services- Youth Program
http://www.acas.org/english/youth.php

Or check out these websites on Photovoice:

http://photovoice.org/
http://www.ivmproject.ca/photo_voice.php

For more info on GAAP:
Gendering Adolescent HIV/AIDS Prevention
www.utoronto.ca/iwsgs/GAAP/index.html

RE-ACT!

Jay and Romeo

Youth Action Network
Gendering Adolescent AIDS Prevention Project

I first met Jay and Romeo at a sexual and reproductive health conference where they were facilitating a rockin' theatre-based workshop on disability and sexuality... I had the pleasure of seeing them work again when they facilitated a Resistance button making workshop on HIV/AIDS stigma and discrimination for the Gendering Adolescent AIDS Prevention project. Their perseverance and commitment continues to amaze me.

Jay and Romeo are two youth facilitators for SprOUT, a project of the Griffin Centre. They also attend Compass, a weekly group founded by Jay.

Project Description

Griffin Centre is a non-profit charitable mental health agency providing flexible accessible services to youth, adults and their families. Our mission is to promote positive change for vulnerable youth and adults with mental health challenges and/or developmental disabilities and their families. We are dedicated to delivering innovative services and developing creative partnerships that enhance lives and communities.

ReachOUT: A creative, inclusive & accessible program for lesbian, gay, bisexual, transgender, transsexual, two-spirit, intersex, queer and questioning (LGBTT2IQQ)youth in north Toronto. Includes drop-in groups, community outreach, counselling, art & skills exchange. We offer a safe space for all youth that reflects the diversity of our queer and trans communities.

Compass is a weekly group for youth labelled with intellectual disabilities to explore sexual and gender identities - including youth who identify as LGBTT2IQQ. The group includes social activities, discussion, movies, art making, outings, interactive workshops, and sexual health information.

SprOUT is a multi-year province-wide project focused on building community with LGBTQ people labelled with intellectual disabilities and their allies. Through trainings provided across the province of Ontario and co-facilitated by LGBTQ people labelled with intellectual disabilities, this project will enhance individual health and improve service access by creating increased capacity for support services to respond to our communities.

Interview Questions

Jay and Romeo – participants of the Sex-Esteem Workshop (Sexual Health and Developmental Disabilities Committee of Waterloo Region)

NAME: Jay and Romeo
AGE: 17 and 24
LOCATION (i.e. Toronto): Toronto, ON
ORGANIZATION/PROJECT NAME: SprOUT, Griffin Centre

How did you get started? What lead you to want to do work around anti-homophobia, anti-transphobia, and sexual health, especially with and for people with intellectual disabilities?

Romeo: Basically I feel there is a lot of homophobia done to these specific groups [people with intellectual disabilities]. People need to be more educated, and I wanted to get my voice heard. I wanted to let people out there know that they have a safe space to go to get support around coming out and dealing with situations.

Jay: I got started for fun; I wanted to meet new people. I wanted to help out other queer youth with a disability, to put myself out there so that people feel supported. I like doing peer support, like helping people out, especially friends. I have been through homophobia and bullying, and so have my friends, so I understand. Even within the [LGBTQ] community I have experienced bashing.

What about your project got you fired up?

Romeo: Getting my message heard and getting the point across. Some people don't have a voice, I wanted to help speak for those people. Also making sure people in schools and parents are educated about homophobia. I love going to workshops, on road trips, seeing new places, doing role plays, and giving definitions of LGBTQ.

Jay: With SprOUT you get to travel, meet new people, and talk to new people that are like you. We try to have as much fun as we can. I learn more about myself, like its okay to be gay. I get knowledge from workshops that I have done. I have more freedom than adults who work here.

Button-Making with SprOUT!
Youth make their own one-of-a-kind buttons that have slogans and/or images that challenge HIV/AIDs stigma and discrimination. This workshop also explores the positive effects that HIV/AIDs has had in our communities. SprOUT workshops take place throughout Ontario and are co-facilitated by LGBTQ people labelled with intellectual disabilities.

Why do you do this work?

Romeo: I love it, it's my passion. I love getting the message across: "Don't hate me cause I'm someone that has an intellectual disability, but respect me for me!"

Jay: It's not for the money; just because I can buy things doesn't make me happy. I get to hang out with new people and youth in general. [Otherwise] I feel like it is hard to meet other people that are LGBTQ and so young. It is better for me working with people closer to my age so that they understand what I am going through as a teenager.

Why use art to educate?

Romeo: To show people who we are and what we do. It can be an outreach tool to get people to come and see what we are doing. The art is fun, so they would like to come to groups that have safe space and do arts and workshops. Shows that it's a place to come chill, hang out, and do workshops. The art helps to reclaim who we are, stop oppression; it all goes back to having your voice heard. It gives people without a voice the chance to speak out and get known in the community. It shows that we are hard working, risk taking, and committed.

Jay: Art is fun, I love doing it and I learn. It is much better than speakers or videos on sex ed; you don't have to sit and listen to people talk. It gives the message "resist homophobia, we are not going to take it." Art can try to show people that gay people are not different; it's who you have sex with.

Do you have any suggestions or tips for your interested in doing community activism work?

Romeo: Just make your voice heard; if this is your dream or passion, never give up. There is always one thing, dreams can come true, no matter how high or low. You can dream big, dream low, but in the end your dream will come true. Never give up, be who you are, and be who you want to be.

Jay: Don't be afraid of who you are, you are the person you want to be. Yo, just have fun, take time, learn new things. The more things you learn, the better you will be.

Number of volunteers: 0
Number of staff involved: 2 co-facilitators
Number of participants: 6-9 participants weekly
Time commitment per week: 5 hrs per week per staff

The group meets on a weekly basis on Thursdays from 4:30pm-7:00pm throughout most of the year and transforms into a weekly full day program from the beginning of July until mid August.

Space Required: Kitchen and meeting room

Fundraising Strategies: Grant applications to foundations as well as municipal and provincial funding programs

Materials Needed: Flipchart and markers for educational workshops, TV and DVD player, Portable Boombox with CD Player

Cost: $25 food budget per week, 2 transit tickets per week per participant

griffin centre
EVERYBODY COUNTS

SprOUT Workshop Activity: Resisting HIV/AIDS Stigma and Discrimination in Our Communities Group Drawing

SprOUT workshop Activity: Resisting HIV/AIDS Stigma and Discrimination in our communities Group Drawing

Make one group image. Think about the following questions and draw or write words that express your feelings and thoughts that are related to each question.

1. What is the difference between stigma and discrimination? (6 min)
2. What are the forms of HIV/AIDS-related stigma and discrimination in your communities? Think about how HIV/AIDS stigma and discrimination affects people differently in your communities based on gender, race, sexual orientation, class, ability, access to health care and gender expression. (6 min)
3. How can we resist HIV/AIDS related stigma and discrimination in our communities? Are there any key images are words that come up for you? (6 min)
4. Go over participants drawings and discuss each question with the group.

For More info on the Griffin Centre:
www.griffin-centre.org

For More info on HIV/AIDS and Disability:
Unfortunately, there are very few HIV/AIDS resources for youth with intellectual disabilities... In fact, my search yielded...none! This is a major gap. Here's one site which addresses the connection between disability and HIV/AIDS, however, it leaves out youth issues and intellectual disability. What's up with that?!?

http://www.thebody.com/content/art13443.html

For more Resources on LGBTQ Youth and Sexuality for youth of colour, check out: *http://www.youthresource.com/living/yoc/index.htm*

Some Definitions

Accessibility = Accessibility refers to ensuring that all people, no matter their race, class, ethnicity etc. have the ability and opportunity to access to health and other social services. In this manual it is also used when talking about art and education. This means that the communication of the messages are not limited by language, class, race and other social identities that may pose barriers to certain communities gaining exposure- all can understand and relate to art.

Disability = A disability is usually referred to as physical or mental. Disabilities are often thought of as something that limits an individual's capacities, however, it needs to be recognized that everyone is different and that individuals with disabilities can have talents. Those with disabilities often face challenges when it comes to sexuality due to real or socially constructed factors that limit sexual expression. People with disabilities are often thought to be asexual, and hence not requiring sexual education or places to talk about sexuality.

Inclusion = Inclusion is the meaningful involvement of members of a community in the decision making process. It ensures that the views, perspectives, and needs of all affected communities are actively involved.

LGBTQ = an acronym referring to lesbian gay, bisexual, transsexual/transgender and queer communities. Q can also stand for questioning. Sometimes, you might see LGBTTIQQ2S which is more inclusive: lesbian gay, bisexual, transsexual, transgender, intersex, queer, questioning, and two spirited.

Homophobia = To be afraid of homosexuality. Those who hold homophobic beliefs often discriminate against homosexuals and treat them in demeaning ways. It works to limit the ability of homosexuals to access equal rights in society, making them at an increased risk for contracting HIV infection. Homophobia can exist on an overt and individual level whereby one person by discriminate towards a person who identifies as homosexual or homophobia can exist in more covert ways in how society may be organized such as around the idea of the nuclear family. The 'ideal' family is viewed to be a male, female and child. Homosexuals in certain countries are not allowed to adopt children.

RE-ACT!

Nadia Alam

Youth Action Network
Gendering Adolescent AIDS Prevention Project

Nadia was one of the first women I interviewed for this manual. Nadia's passion for HIV/AIDS activism was evident from the beginning of our conversation as she spoke about her desire to mix fashion with activism. What Nadia doesn't tell you in this interview is that she was responsible for designing the t-shirts worn by participants in the fashion show, and has created an award-winning short film on her journey as a Muslim woman. Talk about wearing your heart (and politics) on your sleeve! Nadia's stuck out 1.5 years of emails, phone chats and digital requests. She may not have known what she was getting into at the beginning, but having her featured in the manual was certainly worth it on our end!

Project Description

Fashioning Change: A Youth-Inspired Fashion Show

An international collection of organizations display unique and original creations, ranging from "everyday practical" to "fashionably absurd," that reflect and inspire the fight against HIV/AIDS. Hosted by former MuchMusic celebrity Jennifer Hollett.

As part of the presentation at the International AIDS Conference in Toronto, YouthCare organized and hosted a fashion show, where youth had the chance to model their own designs, reflecting the fight against HIV/AIDS. During the Global Village festival, this fashion show encouraged Canadian youth participants to express their views and feelings about the AIDS pandemic in a creative fashion

Interview Questions

NAME: Nadia Alam
AGE: 18
LOCATION (i.e. Toronto): Toronto
PROJECT NAME: Fashion Change

How did you get started? What led you to pursue HIV/AIDS activism?
At age 17 I had an interest in HIV/AIDS while doing a project for a World Issues class. This was the first moment in which I fully understood the current AIDS situation all around the world, as opposed to just Africa.

Also, during this time, I received an e-mail from Verve Girl Magazine's mailing list that there was a fundraising event hosted by YouthCare's Jennifer Hollet that was for anyone who had something to say about the HIV/AIDS situation using fashion as the outlet (to convey a message). This attracted my attention, as I just recently learned about the AIDS epidemic and thought it was my duty to do something about it. This was a perfect place to begin!

Following that, at Marc Garneau Collegiate Institute, my high school, everyone was called to go down to an assembly. This is where I met Jennifer Hollett (former *MuchMusic* VJ), and was introduced to her incredible journey through the northern part of Africa. Her message was about educating the youth and letting them know that they could do something to help!

By meeting her, I got a chance to let her know personally that I was really interested about the project, and that I would definitely do it.

In August of 2006 a group of girls and I got together and came up with an idea for Fashioning Change: A Youth Inspired Fashion Show, a theme of Superheroes to save people from AIDS. We created the message "We can all be heroes. Aid to end AIDS". I designed three t-shirts inspired by three superheroes, Spider(wo)man, Bat(wo)man, and Super(wo)man.

The shirts were showcased by the group of us girls as part of the AIDS Conference 2006, at Yonge and Dundas Square and the Metro Toronto Convention Centre.

This was not the end for me. I felt so motivated that I continued by volunteering my time to Fashion Cares this summer. I'm also working on trying to create a YouthCare group at my campus, Ryerson University.

What about your project got you fired up?
Mostly, I got fired up mainly due to the fashion aspect of it. I couldn't believe that my passion for AIDS activism and my passion for creating fashion were coming together for a great youth-lead project.

Why do you do this work?
I do this work because, more than anything, I want to educate people about something that's not only happening in Northern Africa, but right here in Canada. This issue is occurring right at home and some people don't even know it!

Why art?
I personally am a visual learner. I've always felt motivated by crafts, the fashion industry, and visual art. I feel that if you can grab someone's attention with "THAT'S HOT" printed on your t-shirt, you can grab someone's attention with a message about AIDS on your t-shirt.

Ryan Gosling attracted attention with his "Save Darfur" t-shirts when no one knew the genocide situation in Darfur, Sudan. It's surprising how a simple visual aid can attract attention and allow for people to question a topic and be curious enough to find out what it's about.

Do you have any suggestions or tips for youth who are interested in pursuing HIV/AIDS arts activism models?
Research, ask, get involved, and generate discussion. The more it's talked about, the more you will learn and teach others. A great website from a youth perspective is http://care.ca/youthCARE/.

Anything else?
The experience I had with Fashioning Change was a pivotal moment in my life when I realized, amongst other things, that educating and learning about HIV/AIDS is something I was meant to do.

* * *

BIO

Nadia Alam is 18 years old. Nadia attends Ryerson University for Hospitality and Tourism Management. She lives in East York, Ontario where she works at a community centre part-time as a Special Events and Volunteer Recruitment Coordinator. Her interests include film, photography, writing, sewing, and fashion!

Number of volunteers: 20
Number of staff involved: 2
Number of participants: 20
Time commitment per week: Once a week
For how long?: Two Months!
Space required: A meeting place (we usually sat at an office located on Spadina), where we could follow up on designs, locations, and brainstorm ideas.

Nadia's model rocking her rad designs! From left to right: Arulvizhy Elanko, Nayani Thiyagarajah, Sunita Surendra.

For More Info on YouthCare:
www.care.ca/main/?en&homeYouth

Some Definitions

"Aid to end AIDS" = Aid in the form of money or supplies is often given from governments and non-governmental organizations to countries most affected by HIV/AIDS. While such aid is necessary and can be helpful in both the prevention and treatment in HIV/AIDS, this is not always the case. For example, aid can often be tied to certain ideologies and those who accept aid can be required to use it for purposes dictated to them by the donor or be forced to change policies to gain access to the aid. For example, USAID, a faction of the United States government, donates millions in aid money each year to the fight against HIV/AIDS in Africa. However, USAID condemns the promotion of condoms as an effective prevention measure against the spread of HIV/AIDS. They see the main forms of HIV/AIDS prevention to be abstinence and being faithful to ones relationship partner. There is much controversy and debate around whether this is a realistic strategy and whether the absence of condoms from their comprehensive HIV/AIDS prevention program is actually worsening the situation.

Did you know?!
Many people associate HIV or AIDS with Africa. While certain parts of Africa, such as Sub-Saharan Africa do have high rates of HIV and AIDS, HIV rates are incredibly varied. In fact, according to the 2007 UN Epi report, North America's HIV prevalence rate (0.6%) was listed as higher than North Africa's, including the Middle East (0.3%).

RE-ACT!

Sourav Deb

Youth Action Network
Gendering Adolescent AIDS Prevention Project

I met Sourav at Youth Action Network in the Spring of 2008, where he was taking a break after attending a downtown rally. We talked about his work, the connections between racism and food, and working for change. Because of busy schedules, communication was sparse over the next few months, so I was super happy to bump into them at the Taking Action Project, where he was facilitating an HIV/AIDS workshop for Aboriginal youth in Toronto. As the oldest in the group, this man's been using the language of hip hop, and the culture of change to connect with other youth for over 5 years. Sourav and Stolen From Africa's work is a testament that as youth, we resist in the language, art, and style of our choosing.

NAME: Sourav Deb
AGE: 27
LOCATION (i.e. Toronto): Toronto
ORGANIZATION/PROJECT NAME: Stolen From Africa, MuteScreamz Mentaltainment

Project Description

STOLEN FROM AFRICA is a Toronto-based movement used to promote cultural and historical awareness through education, fashion, music and the arts. We hope to empower society by confronting issues surrounding black/indigenous oppression and humanity as a whole. We are merely people of various ethnicities, who are inspired by the effects of colonialism with aspirations of connecting and learning from the communities in which we live in world wide.

What does "STOLEN FROM AFRICA" mean to you?

Many have viewed the term "STOLEN FROM AFRICA" as controversial, politically incorrect, biased and even racist. Others may view it is as means of empowerment, identity, knowledge and understanding. However you wish to interpret the meaning behind "STOLEN FROM AFRICA", one thing is certain; you will be engaged in a forum of discussion.

The Message:
Our music and our politics speak to a new generation of youth who are looking for more than the clichéd "bling bling" lifestyle and has led to us performing and connecting with a wide variety of artists such as Public Enemy, Dead Prez, Killah Priest, Mathematik, Michie Mee, Maestro and K'Naan. Recently, our organization completed a tour of several Toronto high schools, resulting in filled auditoriums, stunned faculty and hundreds of students becoming aware of many often overlooked issues. In addition to HIV/AIDS, we speak on such overlooked issues as: *Media Awareness, *Cultural Identity, *Our Hidden History, *Peacekeeping, *Materialism, *Gender Roles, and *Family.

> *"By speaking out in the community, bridging the gap between youth and authority and challenging their minds, we can connect with young people from all walks of life and help them better understand their place in their community, their society and in history".*
>
> ***—Sourav Deb***

Interview Questions

How did you get started? What led you to pursue HIV/AIDS activism?
Well when I started using music as a tool for social change, I slowly started getting involved with more hands on politics. Rather than simply speaking change, I became change, I projected change. This process was not only one where we educated and motivated youth, we also have learned a lot during the journey. I spoke at conferences across the country, spoke on MTV, universities, city hall, community centres, high schools to junior schools and I realized one thing, all of our struggles are related. All of our accessibility issues, all of the marginalized aspects of our existence really co-relate to one another.

When we would speak about colonialism, importance of self history, peace keeping, police brutality, sexism, racism, ableism, the stereotypical connotations attached to single moms, to people living with HIV, to the automatic assumptions society places on homeless youth, The response would always be the same, people nodding their heads to my message. So there I had it — I realized how to draw relations between every struggle; therefore, one workshop essentially became the basic framework to all of my workshops.

I received an email one morning from a lady who heard about our workshops, she was from a organization who dealt with children directly/indirectly affected by HIV/AIDS. That was the first focused workshop I have done regarding this issue. The youth were all of African descent and they were between the ages of 11 - 17. After the first workshop, the strength in these children's eyes and the determination in their voices fed my soul. The way they articulated their experiences was amazing. They each made a mask and coloured it, the colour represented different emotions or traits which they later explained to us. We then, as a group, wrote a poem about the masks while incorporating all the meaning behind the colours which were used. The song was eventually recorded by the kids themselves at a studio in the downtown core of Toronto.

Since this workshop, I have always found the need to draw parallels to the way many marginalized people are stereotyped to the way people living directly/indirectly with HIV/AIDS are perceived and pre-judged.

What about your project got you fired up?

We have conducted over 50 HIV-related workshops. The main thing that consistently fires me up throughout each workshop is being able to witness and experience the growing talent in these youth. It amazes me that the most quiet youth in the bunch will end up being one of the most talkative by the end of the sessions. The youth have always created more than I have expected from them. It is always a good spiritual feeling to hear the youth be able to speak their minds and their hearts openly, without discretion, without fear of judgment. Every time I leave a workshop I think to myself, “If these kids are the future, then we will be just fine!!”

Why do you do this work?
I do this work because I have no choice. I see people around me dying because of the lack of self-knowledge and self-worth, spending years in prison often because of the colour of their skin or their religion. I see people even killin' themselves, often because they feel alienated from society. I see women being disregarded by the police as they complain about a sexual assault and in turn find themselves be victimized and deported because of their immigration status. I see my mom and all my friends mothers struggle because of poverty. I see misery all around me, no one is free while others are oppressed.

I also do this type of work because the music industry is a draining machine that leaches on peoples energies. This music industry is built just like the "plantation". Therefore when I do work with the youth, they do the opposite for my spirit, they give me truth, honesty, and a meaning to life.

In short, I was one of these youths that are labeled gangsters, therefore I know what they really are, they are just searching for someone who will listen, someone who will give worth to their opinion. I used to be ready to die just because, but now I ready to live for a cause.

Why art?
To be brief, art is a universal language. For example, I was in India and I saw a man wearing a Tupac t-shirt. Hip hop is a worldwide phenomenon: people from across the world are creating hip hop, hip hop conferences have participants who speak several different languages. This shows you that hip hop is universal. The drum can be found in every culture, it may look a little different, give off a slightly different vibration, it may be called something else, but it is universal.

You can translate visual art and dance in any language, for those two elements of art are like languages in themselves.

Beat boxing is a universal language where we speak to one another in rhythm, much like all music in general.

Art is also a historical technique of teaching. Many First Nations communities have used storytelling, many South Asians have used dance, many Africans used drumming and so forth.

Another reason why art is an important tool in this line of work is because people do not learn in the same way, therefore different approaches should be taken to motivate the youth who are otherwise dazed off by the modern day curriculum structure.

Art is also a great way for the youth to get a sense of community; it shows them the power of art and how in engages everyone around them. Dancing involves team work, writing and recording a song requires team work and co-operation.

Art is a universal language and it will always be one of the most powerful non-traditional youth engagement mechanisms; and engaged youth means youth who are ready to learn.

Do you have any suggestions or tips for youth who are interested in pursuing or already working on HIV/AIDS arts activism?
Be real, be honest and don't always rely on your framework. Sometimes you may have to vibe off the youth and let them somewhat lead the discussions. Youth always smell a lie, so don't sugarcoat anything for them, tell them exactly how it is and they will respect you more.

BIO

Sourav Deb lives in Toronto where he works as a social worker, when not working on Stolen From Africa Projects. He is the founder of Stolen From Africa and MuteScreamz Mentaltainment.

Number of volunteers: 4
Number of staff involved: 4
Number of participants: 12 - 30
Time commitment per no set time (constant work, this is life)
For how long: Since 2003
Space required: Classroom, office space, staircase, park, studio, community centre

For More info on Stolen From Africa:
http://stolenfromafrica.com

Check out SFA's latest project, the film Stolen From Africville: Broken Home, Broken Hearts, a film about Africville (Halifax, NS) – the first black settlement which was abolished by the Canadian Government in 1969:

http://stolenfromafrica.com/stolenfromafricville/the-film/

Some Definitions

Colonialism = Colonialism is a historical concept referring to the control of one nation by another. The controlling nation comes to dominate the resources, labour and markets of the colonial territory and establishes an exploitative relationship with the controlled nation. It was often based on a belief that the ethnic values, morals and culture of one nation is superior to another. Colonialism is often linked to oppression and a major factor in perpetuating the poverty in many of the world's less developed nations. Today, many say that the period of colonialism is over and that we now live in an era of post-colonialism where the majority of nations of the world are free from external rule. While this may be true, there have emerged new ways in which nations of the world are controlled.

For example, when a less developed nation approaches a major money lending institution, such as the World Bank, the loan they secure comes with conditions that have the effect of hindering their development and efforts to alleviate poverty, the goal of taking out the loan in the first place. In addition, loans are given at such high interest rates that the original vale of the loan is repaid several times over and in effect the less developed nation is once again being exploited for the benefit of more developed and powerful nations. This phenomena is called neo-colonialism, meaning new colonialism.

Oppression = When power is used to elevate one social group over another, denying the disadvantaged group of a voice through which to assert their needs. Oppression goes hand in hand with marginalization. People can be oppressed based on race, sexual orientation, gender, faith, ability, age, class, HIV status etc. and because an individual's identity is composed of many different labels each faces oppression from a different constellation of forces. The labels people identify with intersect to define the types and ways they are oppressed and to what extent.

JONATHAN CHHUN

Head & Hands

Keepin' It Real
Sexual education with black youth

"I jokingly say that I'm in recovery from hip hop, it's like being in a domestic violence situation, your home is hip hop, and your man beats you up."

— A black woman (in the documentary* Hip Hop: Beyond beats and rhymes*) explains her mixed feelings towards hip hop culture, referencing the misogynistic themes that have largely replaced positive messages of unity amongst black people since the 1990s.

Hip hop is widely popular across the globe, and is a dominant youth culture in North America. It seems hip hop, as it is portrayed in the media today, is the repetition of centuries old stereotypes about gender roles. Patriarchy, capitalism and white supremacy are ideologies that seem to lurk beneath this multi-million dollar industry. But still, hip hop culture speaks volumes about the experiences of marginalization and oppression faced by black youth. It has also transcended the boundaries of race, ethnicity, gender, class and age. For these reasons, some scholars have argued that hip hop is a culturally relevant framework to educate and to discuss sexual stereotypes and sexuality with youth.

Some aspects of hip hop have been widely criticized, especially the rigid, gendered stereotypes associated with both women and men. The representation of women as sexual objects and "bitches" and men as "thugs" is damaging to youth's sexualities. There is also a side of hip hop that is known to promote community values and challenge conservative views and politics; it is often referred to as old school hip hop.

It is precisely this controversy surrounding hip hop that makes it an excellent medium to discuss issues such as sexuality, gender roles and STIs.

In the context of my studies in Sexology and my internship at Head & Hands, a Montréal-based non-profit community organization, I have created a series of sexual education workshops for black youth aged 12 to 17 years old. The following are some suggestions of subjects to include in sexual health education with black youth, as well as some myths and their answers.

The use of a hip hop song or video clip can be a great way to break the ice and to grab youth's attention. Some examples of artists that convey thoughtful messages include A Tribe Called Quest, Public Enemy, The Roots, Lauren Hill, Lupe Fiasco, Jean Gray, etc. I have personally used, to great effect, a song called "You Never Know" by rapper Immortal Technique. Even though it contains some stereotypes, negative portrayals of sexuality and offensive language, the artist is keepin' it real by talking about adolescent love, sexuality and HIV/AIDS in a very touching manner. The rawness and emotion of this song instantly created a lively discussion about HIV/AIDS and the meaning of sex. It is important to point out and discuss the values expressed in any song, and use the controversy in them to spark youth's attention. The discussion format is highly encouraged and should focus on:

- Stereotypes: our responsibility to discuss and challenge them. Black youth are plagued by even greater stereotyping. The portrayal of women is often even more sexualized, without many examples of successful women. The black man is seen as a basketball player or a woman/money-hungry thug. There is a link between the strong internalization of stereotypes and the age of first intercourse, as well as an increased number of sexual partners, both factors contributing to the high levels of STIs among youth (see Peterson, 2007; Wingwood, 2003).

- The link between capitalist, patriarchal and consumerist North American values and the values expressed in the very commercial side of hip hop should be discussed and explored with youth.

Further critical questions for discussion about hip hop and society include:

- Why so much bling in hip hop? Many mainstream hip hop artists flaunt their goods in a very theatrical, buoyant way. It seems that the American Dream dictates that you should show your power and wealth in a subtle fashion: Ivy League degrees, Italian suits and BMWs. Black people mock this hypocrisy and feel a need to show that they have "made it", despite often being excluded from wealth and power.

- Why is the thug life and misogyny glorified? North America's fascination with sex and violence is strongly linked to hip hop's fascination with those themes: Scarface, James Bond, 50 cent and Tupac share similarities. It seems black people are the targets of far more critics than media conglomerates, although violence and misogyny are central parts of American popular culture and history. Patriarchal values are at the heart of commercial hip hop values.

My experience has shown me that black youth must explore their feelings and opinions about the sexual representation of men and women in hip hop and in society at large. With the very same tool used to disseminate misinformation and stereotypes about the sexualities of men and women of colour, we can reach youth and plant that seed of critical thinking.

* * *

Jonathan Chhun *is a French-speaking Cambodian residing in Montreal. He is finishing his Sexology B.A at UQAM, and is doing his internship at Head & Hands. He is an animator for the Sense Project, Head & Hands' holistic, comprehensive sex education program.*

REFERENCES/ARTICLES FOR FURTHER READING

Hurt, Byron, "Hip hop: Beyond beats and rhymes", DVD, 2006.

Peterson, Shani H., Wingwood, Gina M., Diclemente, Ralph J., Harrington Kathy, Davies Susan, 2007, "Images of Sexual Stereotypes in Rap Videos and the Health of African American Female Adolescents", *Journal of Women's Health*, Vol.16, N.8, p. 1157-1164.

Saddik, Annette J., 2003, "Rap's Unruly Body: The Postmodern Performance of Black Male Identity on the American Stage", *The Drama Review*, N.47, Vol. 4, p.110-127.

Stephens P. Dionne, Few, April L., 2007 "The Effects of Images of African American Women in Hip Hop on Early Adolescents' Attitudes Toward Physical Attractiveness and Interpersonal Relationships", *Sex Roles*, N.56, p.251-264.

Stephens P. Dionne, 2003, "Influence of Female Sexual Scripts Depicted in Hip Hop on African American Young Adolescents Understanding of Sexuality", PhD thesis, Georgia, The University of Georgia, 133 p.

Wingwood, Gina, Diclemente, Ralph J., Bernhardt Jay M., Harrington Kathy, Davies L. Susan, Robillard Alyssa, Hook, Edward W.2003, "A Prospective Study of Exposure to Rap Music Videos and African American Female Adolescent's Health", *American Journal of Public Health*, Vol.93, N.3.

Life is not meant just to build up
our strengths and power,
but also to be in relationships
of love and kindness with others,
where we give life to each other.

– Jean Vanier

CARRIE SINGH

Good for Her

Sexual Health Education and Pleasure Project (SHEPP)

Moving towards a more inclusive sexual education for youth

Working in a sex shop and education centre in Toronto I sometimes feel like a fly Canada's sexual wall. I get to see how savvy people are (or aren't) when it comes to sexuality, the old myths and misconceptions that just won't go away, but more importantly — what people want to know.

As I walk curious customers through a sometimes unfamiliar world, the "oohs" and "ahs" and "oh now that makes sense" reveals a lot about the level of the sex education Canadians enter into adulthood with. Of course everyone comes armed with a different level of knowledge, but what seems clear to me is that if you want to be educated about healthy sexuality, it must come through your own personal journey of exploration and educating oneself through a variety of conventional and not-so-conventional resources. For some this may make perfect sense — after all, sex is a highly personal subject that should be kept in the bedroom. Or should it?

Like many of my customers, my "real" sex education was not learned in school. Before I got this job, no one told me that lube could make my sexual endeavours safer and more pleasurable. Intercourse appeared to be the only sexual activity between partners that mattered or constituted "real sex". And I was always told to use condoms, but I wasn't told how to negotiate condom use or how to account for the realities of my social location. The sex ed. I learned in school gave me the very basic of knowledge, and being from a South Asian-Carribbean family, the topic of sex was almost nonexistent. So what if I never took this job and learned the things I did? Would my sexual relationships look any different? And would I be able to make the empowered decisions that I do today? Would I have the knowledge to protect myself the way I am able to now? I feel extremely privileged, for I have access to knowledge that protects my health and allows me to enjoy a fulfilling sexual life.

Despite the changing demographic face of Canada and emerging trends, few educational programs have changed to address the needs of youth of colour or employ culturally competent methods. Young women of colour are experiencing increasing rates of HIV and Sexually Transmitted Infections while schools continue keep sex education to a conservative minimum. As a student in the 1990's, I don't remember receiving much more than an anatomy lesson in gym class and a being told to always use a condom. Speaking from my own cultural reality, it is assuming a lot to inform young girls and women to simply get their male partner to wear a condom. Traditional methods of sex education assume a generality of experiences based on a white, heteronormative standard. This disregards many realities for youth, including the cultural and religious values and norms that impact sexual behaviour and self-image, as well as social location.

Canadians of all backgrounds are informed by Western, patriarchal notions about sexuality. Though Canada is diverse in population, many cultural norms and practices have largely been eroded in favour of a white, European, Christian value system. A highly gendered depiction of sexuality, moral judgments around "promiscuous behaviour" and the invisibility of people of colour and sexuality have helped to distort many diverse and inclusive expressions of sexuality.

Furthermore, many communities of colour experience disproportionate access to social, economic, medical, educational and community resources. When it comes to sex education in Toronto, this has seemed to manifest itself in a glut of youth services in the downtown core but a complete lack outside of the mainstream.

Technically a youth from the suburb of Scarborough can jump on public transit to try and access the wealth of services in the downtown core. But that is assuming this person has the extra bus fare to spare, is aware of the services outside of his or her community, and believes that they would be included in such services.

This is why the Sexual Health, Education & Pleasure Project (SHEPP) is such an exciting project to be a part of. SHEPP was started by members of Good For Her (a sex shop in Toronto specializing in women's sexuality) and is currently run by volunteers committed to equitable sex education. The goal of the project is to provide accessible, inclusive and empowering sex education to youth, with a focus on youth of colour communities. While sex education in Canada has been very basic in general, diverse communities have traditionally been short-changed by mainstream models. SHEPP aims to contextualize sexual experiences and understand the current issues that are relevant to youth. Reflecting the populations we serve in our facilitators, finding out directly from youth what they want to learn about and using their language are some of the ways we are trying to make sex education for youth of colour more accessible. One of our most important strategies is outreach. We want to go out and find the youth who traditionally may not have felt comfortable walking into a community centre or health clinic. We want to learn from youth how we can create new and more inclusive models of education.

Working in a sex shop I get to educate people on an individual basis, listening to where they are at, gauging their comfort level and tailoring my approach to their needs. We may not have such a luxury on a wider educational level, but assuming that a single program or single approach will meet everyone's needs will probably do little more than continue an out-of-date method.

* * *

Carrie Singh *has a Bachelor of Social Work from Ryerson University with a background in harm reduction and street outreach. She currently coordinates the Sexual Health, Education & Pleasure Project (SHEPP) and works at Good For Her, a women-friendly sex shop and education centre in Toronto.*

ALEXANDRA LOOKY

Sexual Education Version 2.0

As a young woman coming from Togo, sexual education in North America is what I find to be a privilege. This luxury however still lacks in various ways such as the approaches used in terms of the material, nature and content of the messages to convey as well as the origins, values and social norms of the audience these messages are destined to. I therefore would like to offer my opinion on how to approach this sensitive and challenging matter.

In terms of my background, I have been exposed to various cultures since I was a child and therefore, to varying views and methods when approaching/addressing the topics of sex education/sexual behavior and practices.

I received my sexual education in grade 8 (so I was 13) and at the time I was not yet a resident of Canada. I was living in my country of birth attending a French school. I am stressing the latter as I received my education modeled on that of France and not on that of the Togolese education system. To my knowledge, sex education is still not yet offered in public schools although Togo has come a long way in its HIV/AIDS campaign. Sex education back then just consisted of the biology of the reproductive systems (it was done in biology class and hardly lasted more than a couple of class sessions) and the contraceptive measures available.

When I moved in Canada, I received along with my housemates in boarding school in Quebec, a relatively similar sex education talk with the visual aid of a condom being rolled on a banana. Condoms were always available at the infirmary. The main problem, I quickly realized was that although the subject of STIs/STDs was broached mentioned, it was barely so done, all the focus remaining on ways to prevent teen pregnancies and HIV infections.

A lot of what I know about sexual health, STIs, I have learnt myself through personal curiosity. I quickly realized at an early age I was being limited. My identity implies I have been exposed to a different gender script and expected sexual conduct, being a woman, a black woman, and an African woman and coming from a world where women still have subservient positions whether it be in terms of rights or the set mentality. I personally also know a little more because of my science background.

As a consequence, I feel like I have to read every pamphlet I can get my hands on to really know about diseases. I am aware that those pamphlets are summarized and worded in laymen's terms for accessibility. Some pamphlets do a better job than others. I remember that at university, the pamphlets were more descriptive and straightforward and addressed a much larger variety of STIs.

I have therefore provided below my thoughts and contributions on how to approach sexual education, especially in Canada, which represents today a significant mixture of communities which social norms greatly differ from the Canadian white heterosexual man and woman.

- I am under the impression that HIV is considered the extreme of STIs and therefore less attention is given to the other STIs. I believe it is important to put equal emphasis on all STIs and remind the reality of all those infections and consequences. STIs should not be regarded according to the availability of treatment but according to the damage it causes to our bodies and the eventual short and long term consequences. For example: although antibiotics are available to cure syphilis, it may not be treatable at if not treated in the first stages and eventually fatal while affecting the brain (and behavior) in the process.

- The average Canadian is still ignorant when it comes to sexual and reproductive health but is living in a country where countless resources are readily available. People, including teenagers, seem to be only obsessed with what is treatable and not treatable and the public health system often feeds that obsession. **Get the facts straight**. For example there is no cure for herpes, only treatment options are available once you are infected.
- Remind people that STIs are on the rise in North America, particularly in heterosexual relationships, especially HIV, because of people misconceptions on what is treatable and so on and attitude towards sexual behavior.
- What is risky behavior? What is considered risky behavior? How does one define risky behavior?
- Look at our attitude in long-term committed relationships. Being safe does not mean going on the pill. I believe we should encourage people to adopt a habit of their own once engaging in committed relationships.
  - → What are the tests one should go for before deciding to remove the barrier of protection (condoms)?
  - → Is a HIV test the only required test?
  - → What else should we test or screen for?
  - → How often should a couple get tested?
  - → Should we really get rid of condoms usage even in long-term committed relationships?
  - → Should preventing pregnancy be the only eventual responsibility/concern of a heterosexual couple?
- Sexual hygiene and sexual health such as regular pap-smears or visits to the gynecologist should not be a 40-year-old woman's advice only.
- Sex education and recreational drugs: how does the influence of drugs change/affect our judgments and our actions? Do not hesitate to be specific starting with the most common drug available: alcohol.
- Pornography and its sources: this one is particularly dear to me. Pornography represents a serious danger to our people for several reasons but mostly for the distorted reality, misconceptions and preconceived notions. It is now the immedi-

ate tool youth uses to educate itself, especially young males. In addition, it causes a greater danger to women, who throughout history have had their sexual behavior dictated and pornography perpetuates those ideas. Please note I am not condemning pornography itself, but I am condemning the set and often erroneous ideas that the mainstream porn industry instill in the viewers. Viewers should learn to distinguish between the fiction and reality.

- Virtual and/or cybersex chat rooms…
- Music and sex and how some genres of music objectify human beings: for example, hip hop music and the commonality of black women being objectified, disrespected/treated as "bitches"; hip hop mainstreaming to other cultures and carrying those negative messages. Hip hop is not the only type of music that has this kind of considerable consequences.
- Make sexual education and sexual health a credited course offered over several years. Offer evaluations, tests, multiple choice questions, considering many students are motivated by grades; make those evaluations count towards their final average, and students might be as a result eager to find out more.
- Present the information with research activities. Have the students research and find out about diseases or sex education and have them present the material. I am quite aware that talking about sex can make many uncomfortable, but again sex is what youth undeniably is interested in.
- Ask the student/youth what they wish in particular to know about a certain topic and find out about it.
- Inform youth about the resources currently available: such as WHO, UNAIDS, links to Canadian government...
- Posters — there can never be enough of them. A picture is definitely worth a thousand words. Be aggressive if need be about the message. HIV ads often do not hesitate to do so. Inform youth about the resources currently available: such as WHO, UNAIDS, Canada government links... What really is lacking is our attitude toward our concept of sex.

It feels like sex education always has been the thing schools have to do in order to control/ reduce teenage pregnancy and HIV infection by giving the basic preventive speech. I believe more proactive ways of teaching can be done without having to offend one's person, religious and cultural beliefs.

Different suggested approaches:

- Challenge the student to set their standards about their sexual life.
- Do not impose but educate and discuss. The audience needs to know they are not being talked at but talked to.
- Ask them their differences and opinions about important concepts such as gender identity, reproduction, sexual identity and sexual orientation. Ask them to define those terms in their own words as an exercise. If the maturity of students is a concern, present the material over several years.
- If feasible also discuss societal norms and gender roles and how it may affect the sexual activities of people, and teenagers in particular preconceptions, stereotypes, and assumptions.
- Teach them the difference about sexual orientation, gender identity, reproduction and so on.
- Discuss further the definition of a sexual act; what are the limitations, what is not considered a sexual act...? Is a sexual act automatically/strictly for reproductive purposes? If not, should the same standards be applied in every situation on what should or should not be allowed?
- Do not focus the sexual education on intercourse only. Talk about other ways to express one sexually and the safety/risks involved. For example, fingers: great to use but remember if there are any cuts to protect yourself from infections such as hepatitis…
- What is rape? Who can be raped? Can women be considered rapists? Rapes are not only perpetrated by men. Women are rapists and women can rape women. How to speak about it. The repercussions on one lying about being raped.
- Always do a LGBT part and ensure students are aware of the basic terminology.
- It is also important to teach preventive measures from STIs to LGBT. That is to teach ahead of time, the options two people of the same sex have to protect themselves. I wish I had known and was taught the importance of dental dam or the alternative to dental dam such as the male condom.

Obviously this is a very sensitive subject to many. One can always choose to present basic information and remind the student that more information is available upon request. There is for instance a big misconception with both heterosexual and LGBT communities that lesbians need very little protection. Many women engaging in sex with the same sex are not aware of their risks, particularly HPV, hepatitis and herpes.

- Another sensitive topic is anal sex; aside from LGBT who gets advice? People know very little in how to engage in safe anal sex both in terms of infections and the possible harm if not done properly.
- Again, discuss how male dominated societies affect sexual practices/behavior and may cause us to engage in unsafe or

March For Women's Lives, 2004

risky behavior. Is Canadian society still considered a male dominated society? We still have for example the problem of double standards. Another example would be to regard oral sex as not being sex at all, or to deny the risks of oral sex performed on a woman. The average heterosexual usually does not shop for dental dams at the same time as condoms.
- Promote the female condoms (or femidoms) and its accessibility: If the government could further stress its use, prices might go down and be more affordable and represent the female tool of protection. Offer female condoms more as a common method of protection for anal sex, especially among men engaging in sex with men. Consider renaming the female condom to make it more accessible to both genders.
- Really stress the importance of educating males and young males at that and teaching them about safe and healthy sexual behaviors which are really lacking.

Canadian institutions need to understand about and take into account the fact that we are conveying messages to an audience that comes from different communities when addressing matters such as sex education. This includes addressing the following points or using the following techniques:

- social norms,
- Sex being taboo
- Use of layman's terms when addressing people about sexual education.
- Address people so that they don't feel talked at but rather talked to.
- Remind audiences their sets of values/beliefs are still being respected.
- In areas/communities where women are expected to fill subservient social positions and thus have no say in their sexual alternatives or choice of sexual partners: educate the women about the available tools, they should be offered options in terms of protection and birth control other than the male condom. A lot of people where I am from do not know about the femidom or the morning after pill.
- Remember that the use of the white male and white female as the standard in sex education is no longer a good or viable model.

- Finally, sex education should not be limited to youth only. Public health should mainstream it to the point where adults of different ages do not hesitate to find out a little more than the typical speech of how to use a condom.

What we really need to work on is our attitude towards and concept of sex. It feels like sex education always has been the thing schools have to do in order to control/ reduce teenage pregnancy and HIV infection by giving the basic preventive speech. I believe more proactive ways of teaching can be implemented without having to offend one's personal, religious and cultural beliefs.

On a personal note, being a woman in this North American society, women need to make the extra effort in recognizing the social norms set in place for them when it comes to sex and learn to set their own standards. Only then, will they would learn to take care of and protect themselves. Men in turn should challenge themselves about their understanding of/behaviours towards sexuality as well.

* * *

Alexandra Looky *is a 25-year-old black woman who has been living in Canada for the past ten years. As a native of Togo (West Africa), she attended French educational institutions until the age of 14 when she moved to Canada to pursue secondary and post-secondary education. She graduated with a B.Sc in Biochemistry in 2005 from the University of Waterloo. She now lives in Toronto, where she works and volunteers as a research assistant.*

ALLYSHIP

JESSICA YEE

Allyship and Youth

What does it mean to be an ally?

For starters, being an ally does not mean that boundaries do not need to be set. Being an ally does not protect you from being in a situation where there is a conflict of interest, or where you are unsure about how to act in the best interests of the person or community.

In short, it is not a get-out-of-jail free card, and if you are prepared to take on this role, please don't take it lightly.

Often times we are confronted with the word "ally" when in dealings with communities that are not our own. Various communities have been using this term for quite some time, while others are now beginning to question whether or not it applies to them. In my opinion, the right to self-determination is paramount to keep in mind within any community when deciding whether or not you want allies, and considering what the result of doing so might look like.

Truth be told, many of us tend to take on the title of "ally" quite automatically, without prior consultation or consent from the community itself. As in "I'm working in allyship with (insert name) and I'm doing (insert action)". Even if we don't say it, we sort of assume we're already an ally before we've even begun to have the conversation with ourselves on what it actually means.

Here is a textbook definition for "ally" in the standard "diversity" optimism-speak:

> "An ally is a member of a dominant group who rejects the dominant ideology and takes action against oppression out of a belief that eliminating oppression benefits everyone." *Teaching for Diversity and Social Justice* edited by Maurianne Adams, Lee Anne Bell and Pat Griffin (Routledge Press, 1997).

So can you be an ally without being part of the dominant group? Is this only about working in partnership with the minority? I think it's both; and when we begin to talk about youth and allyship, many intersections and parallels between the two can be made.

Youth is a community all on its own. This is again my own perspective and in stating so I do not think it should mean that we are hung out to dry all on our own. It means that at our age, we live a different reality than adults although we may have different likes, aspirations, and needs that have to be considered and respected accordingly. Although not always true 100% of the time, age does dictate many things about what various aspects of our lives are going to be like, both legally and socially speaking.

More importantly though, recognizing youth as its own community means that we also recognize that we have our own rights and deserve the opportunity to work within ourselves to find the best solutions to the issues we're facing. We certainly need help, but we need to be the stewards of the information going out about us. And more often than not, we have not been given this opportunity we are rightfully owed.

Seventy percent — maybe even more — of youth programs out there these days are not actually being led or directed by youth. Credible and decades-old research shows that peer education is not only extremely effective, it's vital to the success of anything that has to do with youth. We need concrete, sustainable avenues for youth to become involved — not tokenized, volunteer-only, or after-the-fact opportunities.

So if you want to be an ally with us as youth, here are some things you need to do:

- Take full responsibility for conferred authority.
- Use what we learn although these ways we have not been rewarded in the past.

- Accept efforts to collaborate with youth in different positions who may be exhibiting signs that they want to get involved
- Have the willingness to be vulnerable to criticism from us, to ask for help and to make mistakes.
- Be courageous enough to discuss and challenge your own prejudices.

When addressing the various levels of equity you are seeking in teaching or designing sex or designing sex education, as youth of colour, it is critical to fully intersect our age with our race, and not pretend that a one size fits all model is always going to be effective. it is critical to interesect age with race. This action list provides some insight to abide by:

- ✔ Evaluate efforts to dismantle racism and ageism by the actual results rather than the intentions.
- ✔ Remember the ubiquitous nature of racism and ageism.
- ✔ Seek out and support leadership consistently from young people of colour when you teach.
- ✔ Take a long-term view. Plan educational strategies accordingly.
- ✔ Assess power. Who is receiving and giving attention? How is power being expressed?
- ✔ Do your homework.
- ✔ Take your risks, not other people's. Interventions may inadvertently result in increased oppression for those most vulnerable. Enter when invited. Don't wait until major crises come about to name the ageism and/or racism you see.
- ✔ Invite conflict.
- ✔ Avoid isolation. Work at developing communities of resistance with us.
- ✔ Don't demand congratulations from young people of colour.

The following section of this issue of *Our Schools / Our Selves* is written by people who have identified themselves as allies both in age and in race.

Jessica Yee *is the editor of this issue of Our Schools / Our Selves*

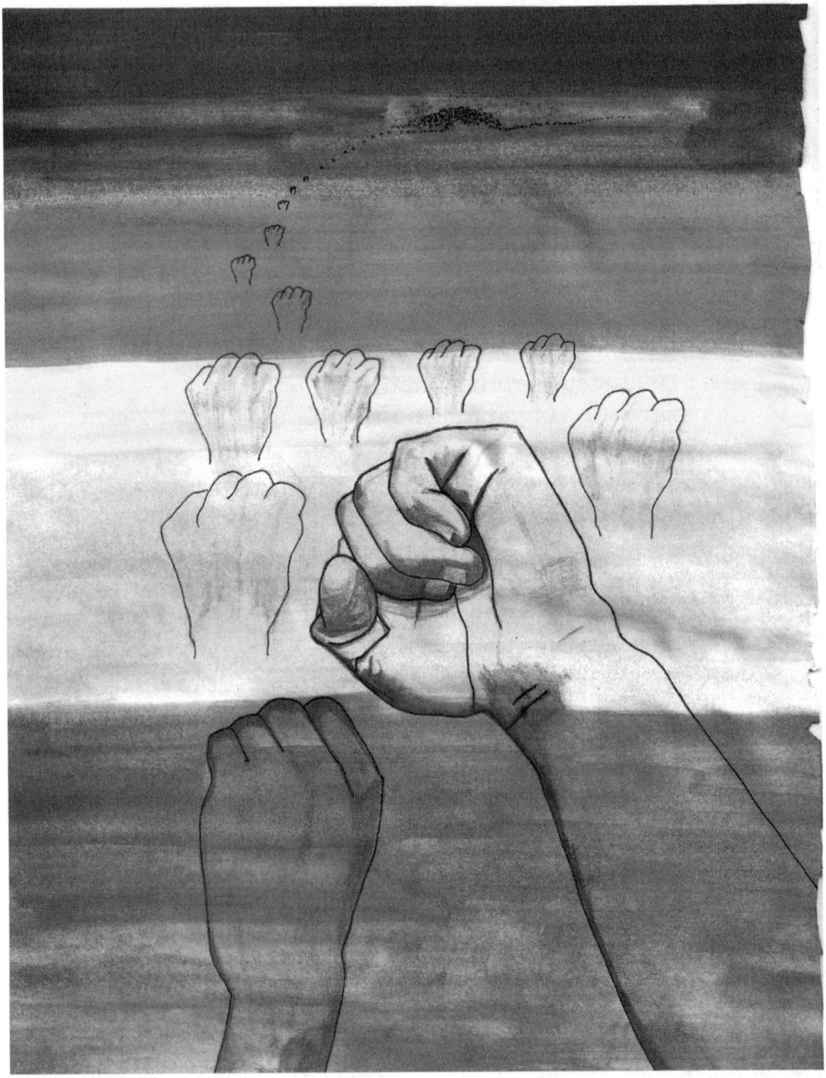

Jennifer Yee

sexuality in color

writing outside the lines at scarleteen

Sexuality in Colour at Scarleteen

Coordinated by HEATHER CORINNA

Newsflash: I'm white. Who cares, right?

Well, I do. Because for one thing that means with the work I do is that I hear it, see it, compile it, write it all through the lens of a white person. I can be as mindful, sensitive and careful as I want, but it still doesn't change that fact.

By all means, I do my research and do everything I can to be sure that the content at Scarleteen is as inclusive as possible: after all, I'm not a heterosexual person either, a male person, nor a young person for that matter, but I think I do okay when it comes to being inclusive for those groups here. And sure, I grew up with a parent who worked for the Civil Rights Movement, have always lives in very integrated, urban areas, and with a taught and learned sensitivity for bias in my world and in myself. Much of my background has been a big help to me when it comes to keeping my eyes open in terms of racial issues, and knowing that when it comes to pretty much everything, race does matter and isn't a non-issue.

But know what that doesn't change? My own race, and my experiences in my life and every single day being that race. I'm still white, and I'm still a white person who writes on sexuality, body image, reproductive health, gender and sexual identity, relationships and sexual politics through my white lens and with certain privileges my colour alone nets me.

Even if you have no personal experience yourself being of colour, or don't talk to people of colour in your life about these issues, statistics alone make very clear that race (and, more to the point, how different races are treated and valued) and our perception of race changes things. HIV and unplanned pregnancy has hit women of colour harder than white women, for instance. Contraceptive and sexual health access can often be tougher for those of colour. Being gay, lesbian or bisexual can play out differently being of colour and in communities of colour. I can see all of those things in the work that I do. I can read about all of those things in journals or newspapers. I can cer-

From the collection by Kangaswaran Nigharamingham

tainly feel empathy, compassion and upset about racial imbalances... but what I can't do is acutely feel and experience those things the way my brothers and sisters of colour do and can. That's not a minor quibble: it's major.

Hearing about those experiences from people of colour, unfiltered, is not as accessible to everyone as it should be.

That given, we're rolling out a new blog series here at Scarleteen where writers of colour have a highly visible space to write on all of these issues and more. We've got a handful of excellent activists, bloggers and Scarleteen users and volunteers ready to tell it like it is; to illuminate, inform and educate. We're thrilled to have this opportunity to provide a space in alignment with one of the core aims we've always had at Scarleteen, which is to assure that as much room is made here for people to talk about their own experiences and to represent themselves as there is for people to be talked about and represented by others.

Our hope is that if you are of colour, you'll find some communion in these pieces, some empowerment and a whole lotta "Hell, yeah." If you're not, we hope that reading these pieces might bump up your awareness, make you think about things you haven't considered before, or start to think — and maybe behave — differently than you did before you read them. We're hoping that some of the issues and perspectives this series brings to light get seen and heard by those who really need to see and hear them, and that they will help to foster positive change and a greater spirit of compassion and unity. We want to open a window with the hope it opens more doors.

Scarleteen's commitment to feminist sex education: it's definitely about race too!

Feminist sex education:

- Emphasizes, for all sexes and genders, autonomy, personal responsibility, full and active consent, sexuality in the holistic context of a whole, well-rounded life, self-esteem, nonsubordination and nonviolence, safety, health , happiness and pleasure and very real equality in sexuality, in which equal voice and accord are given to and issues from any and all partners in sexual partnerships and sexual activity.
- Operates under the given that members of any sex, gender, race, sexual orientation or class have an inalienable, inarguable right to the complete, inarguable ownership of their own, individual bodies and desires, and that sexuality and sexual pleasure is a positive and valuable experience in its own right, not merely or only a side effect of reproduction,

health, biology or romance.

- Recognizes women's sexual desires and sexuality as complete on their own, rather than as an answer to or product or adjunct of male sexuality, male sexual partnership or marriage, as well as acknowledging a wide diversity of sexual desire, experience and identity amoung women.
- Recognizes the bodies and genitals of all people as active, engaged parts of a whole, rather than passive or as object.
- Understands and presents sexual activity, with or without partners, as a choice, not a requirement ro obligation. Encourages consent as active, not passive: not as a not-no or compliance, but as a complete, informed and enthusiastic yes, and encourages open, honest communication in all sexual activities and with all sexual partners.
- Is pro-choice, supporting the right of women to have — as men do — complete sovereignity over their bodies at all times, including during pregnancy, and equally supporting the right of women to choose abortion, adoption or parenting — whichever is best for them by their own determination — in the event they become pregnant. Supports the use of, and encourages complete access to, contraception, safer sex and preventative, holistic sexual healthcare for all, and the position that public policies for women should not be made by men.
- Does not treat gender or sex as binary, and acknowledges gender as constructed, not essential or assigned.
- Recognizes the strong and pervasive effect of cultural and personal sex and gender roles on the individual and interpersonal sexuality, and educates readers about those roles and their right to choose sex and gender roles which are desired, not merely assigned. Addresses cultural inequalities of sex and gender which effect sexuality, such as the effects of commodifying women's bodies, the glortification of male-on-female or male-on-male sexual violence, objectifcation of women, other minorities and sexuality in the media, economic divides, the greater sexual burdens women bear, the greater rates of sexual abuse and rape of women, as well as the detrimental effects of patriarchy upon men, male sexuality, identity and relationships.
- Acknowledges the reality of sexual and other interpersonal abuse and violence and works to counter and prevent those

abuses amoung all sexes and genders, as well as recognizing that many women have survived these abuses, and that this needs be a consideration with sexuality education and understanding of human sexuality.
- Presents partnered sex broadly, acknowledging the wide array of sexual activities which may be "real" partnered sex, not merely heterosexual intercourse. Presents female sexual anatomy more broadly than as to pertain only to heterosexual intercourse or reproduction.

* * *

Scarleteen *provides sex and sexuality education, information and advice for millions of young adults, parents and allies. Scarleteen — often the most highly ranked teen sex education website online — is owned and operated by Heather Corinna and a handful of international volunteers, and currently serves from 20,000 - 30,000 teens and young adults, as well as parents and educators, every day of the year. While some adults also use Scarleteen to glean sexuality information for themselves, Scarleteen is compiled and written for a young adult population, primarily based in the information that population directly asks us for, and much of our information is more appropriate for teens and young adults than for older adults.*

www.scarleteen.com

SARAH FLICKER, ADRIAN GUTA and ROBB TRAVERS

Where Are Toronto Youth Getting Sexual Health Information?

Rates of sexually transmitted infections have been on a slow and steady increase for the last 10 years amongst Toronto's teens. Due to a number of social and biological factors — teens are particularly vulnerable to poor sexual health outcomes. But there are lots of things we can do to reverse this trend. Our research team has spent the last several years mobilizing a youth-lead response.

The aim of the Toronto Teen Survey (TTS) is to gather information from youth on assets, gaps and barriers that currently exist in sexual health education and services and use the information to develop a city-wide strategy to increase positive sexual health outcomes for diverse Toronto youth. What is unique about our research is that teens are integrally involved in all stages of the TTS project from design to implementation and dissemination. From the outset, our goal has been to work in partnership with youth to develop teen-friendly research protocols and interventions. Our youth advisors were recruited from partner agencies within the city, including community and recreation centers, supportive housing organizations, and child protection services with special attention focused on seeking out youth who often are not able to access these sorts of opportunities. To facilitate participation, we were able to cover their transportation costs, and provide snacks and honoraria for participation.

Our youth advisory members received training on topics related to qualitative and quantitative methodologies, sexual health, anti-oppression analysis and the social determinants of health. While no short training programme can be expected to create "expert" survey developers, our intention was to provide the Youth Advisory Committee with enough of an introduction to critically engage with these issues, and draw on their own expertise. With training and support from the research team, they were able to develop a sophisticated and nuanced survey tool that we then distributed to an "expert review panel" and pilot tested to ensure validity.

Our youth advisors were adamant about their desire to have an educational component for survey respondents to answer any immediate sexual health questions they may have following the survey. They did not feel it was adequate to simply administer the TTS, but that the researchers had a responsibility to make the experience educational and informative for respondents. We heeded their advice. Between December 2006 and August 2007, we conducted 90 workshops in community based settings and collected 1,200 surveys from a diverse cross-section of youth. They visited afterschool drop-in programs, shelters, summer camps, community centres, group homes and other community spaces where youth congregate.

Over and over again we heard from our community partners that the peer-approach we adopted was successful in opening up honest dialogue with other youth around sexual health. We also heard from our Youth Advisory Committee that they had become knowledge brokers at schools and in their communities. Many have expressed interest in continuing on in the area(s) of research and health promotion. And many have left us for university.

The Youth Advisory Committee has been both the face and the soul of the TTS. As a result of their involvement we garnered important data about youth access to sexual health resources. What is unique about our sample is that it is the largest community-based youth sample of its kind in Toronto, Canada's most diverse urban centre. Some of the highlights include:

- 85% of our sample were from racially diverse communities of colour;
- 33% were born outside of Canada;
- 17% report a disability
- 7% identified as lesbian, gay, bisexual, queer or questioning;
- 68% had never been to a clinic for any sexual health reasons
- Youth identified wanting more information on healthy relationships, sexual pleasure & HIV as top priorities!

Leading Together, Canada's HIV/AIDS blueprint strategy, identifies youth as a prevention priority, with a commitment to ensuring that by 2010, at least 95% of 15 to 24 year olds are able to reduce their vulnerability to HIV infection. The strategy recommends age-appropriate information, youth-led initiatives, and the direct involvement of youth serving-agencies in the development of HIV prevention resources and interventions. Despite the existence of the strategy, youth surveyed in the TTS are facing barriers to accessing information which meets their sexual health needs.

Are Toronto's youth receiving sexual health education?

We asked youth if they have received sexual health classes or workshops in: elementary school, high school, youth groups, religious groups, or other places. Overall, the vast majority of youth we surveyed (92%) checked off one or more of the above options. We classified these youth as receiving "some form" of sexual health education. 32% of youth only received sexual health education in one location, and 60% received sexual health education in multiple locations. Between the ages of 13-15, just over 90% have received some form of sexual health education, which increases slightly between the ages 15-16 to 91.5%, and again to 93.4% of youth by the age of 17 or older. Most of the Canadian-born youth we surveyed report having received sexual health education in elementary school (67%) and high school (61%), followed by through other youth groups (39%), and religious groups (6%).

While the majority of participating youth (92%) are receiving "some form" of sexual health education, it is noteworthy that 8% have not received any at all. This means that either youth are not being offered this information at any of these locations, are missing the window when the curriculum was covered, or do not remember having received this information.

While this high percentage of education penetration suggests public health success, this finding is not particularly surprising considering that sexual health education is a mandated part of the Ontario curriculum. Nevertheless, it is important to point out that this widespread coverage speaks merely to quantity rather than quality of this information. It is also important to remember the 8% that are being missed.

Immigration plays a determining role in sexual health education access, especially for youth in the school system. By the age of 18, 97% of Canadian-born youth we surveyed have received some sexual health education, whereas newcomer youth (those in Canada less than three years) have received less depending on length of residency. Immigrant youth living in Canada for more than four years "catch up" to their Canadian-born counterparts. By the age of 18, they have received similar levels of sexual health education.

However, compared to Canadian-born teens, newcomers in Canada three years or less, had slightly lower levels of sexual health education at age 13 and significantly lower rates by the age of 18. (Only 76% of newcomer 18 year olds had received sex ed anywhere). These findings have important implications for Ontario's sexual health education curriculum, as our data suggest that more recent newcomers (especially those entering Canada in higher grades) may altogether miss the required sexual health education in elementary and early high school years.

Where do youth go when they have a question about sexual health?

Overall youth are most likely to talk to their friends and professionals.

We asked Toronto teens "where do you go when you have a sexual health question?" Young women are more likely (47.9%) to turn to professional services (including physicians, nurses, pharmacy, and clinical/community health centres) compared to young males (36.5%). Similarly, more young women (37.1%) rely on the mass media (books, magazines, TV, movies or the internet) compared to young males (27.1%). Finally, more young women (62.1%) rely on their peers (friends and siblings) compared to young men (41.3%), and their siblings (females, 24.4%) compared to 14% of males.

We asked Toronto teens "where they would like to go when they have a sexual health question?" There were few differences between young women and men, with 55% of females and 51% of males wanting to consult professionals. Similarly, 34% of females and 30% of males would like to access the mass media for information. While information/phone lines were accessed by 17.5% of females and 17.3% of males (see table), more would like to use these services (34% of females and 30% of males, respectively. Service providers thought that youth are not accessing these services because they are confused about their mandates (e.g., "do they answer sex questions?") and potential concerns over the duty to report (i.e., "will they trace my call?").

It is also important to note that youth from different ethnoracial backgrounds make different decisions about how they get their questions answered. White youth were more likely to access all sources when they had a question about sexual health than any other group. Black youth were least likely to access any source.

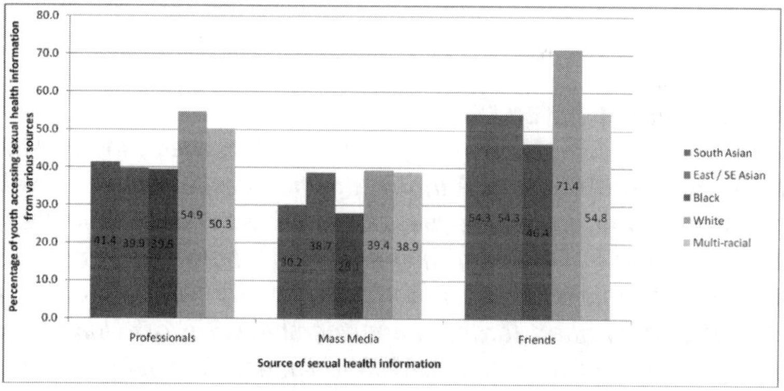

What can we do about this?

Percentage of youth accessing sexual health information by source and ethno-racial diversity

What can we do about this?

As adults and allies, we have a responsibility to make sure that youth have the information they need to make healthy decisions about sex. This means providing information in multiple locations and in multiple formats to reach youth with age-appropriate content that is frank, useful, accessible and culturally appropriate.

For youth that experience heightened barriers to accessing information, we need to redouble our efforts. One strategy might be to make sex ed a requirement every year in school. Another strategy might be to imbed sexual health programming in other locations where youth naturally congregate (eg sports or drama clubs). Since teens seem to want to talk to their friends most, a third option is to ramp up peer training programs. All of these are good ideas that are not mutually exclusive. What is clear is that we need to do a better job. I would like to conclude with a quote from one of our youth advisors — when asked why he chose to participate in our research project — he said "At first I thought it was a great opportunity to get paid, meet girls and talk about sex. But now I know it is so much more." When opportunities are created for youth to meaningfully engage, they rise to the challenge.

* * *

ACKNOWLEDGEMENTS

We thank our team of investigators: Sarah Flicker, June Larkin, Jason Pole, Robb Travers, Adrian Guta and Hazelle Palmer, as well as Susan Flynn, Crystal Layne, our Youth Advisory Committee, and the entire TTS team for their dedication, hard work, and contributions to this project. The Toronto Teen Survey is a project of Planned Parenthood Toronto in partnership with York University, The University of Toronto and Wilfred Laurier University. Toronto Public Health is a collaborator. The Canadian Institutes of Health Research and the Ontario HIV Treatment Network have funded this work; support was also garnered from the Wellesley Institute and the Centre for Urban Health Initiatives.

The Roots of Healing by Sasha Maracle

growingminds
The Power of Learning
MTS
The Manitoba Teachers' Society
mbteach.org

STAR IN YOUR OWN STORIES IS A SUCCESS STORY

CHEE MAMUK

Star in Your Own Stories is a success story. It is a creative, engaging sexual-health project that allows Aboriginal youth to use their voices. This collaborative project has run three years in a row bringing together Chee Mamuk, Aboriginal Program, BC Centre for Disease Control, the STI/HIV Outreach Program, BC Centre for Disease Control and Good Company Communications, a new media company, to work with Aboriginal youth from various BC Nations.

The project-team worked with youth for two-and-a-half days covering health issues such as HIV/AIDS, Sexually Transmitted Infection (STI) information, healthy sexuality, condom use, self esteem, how to create positive messaging, and camera equipment instruction. The project-team then transitioned the youth to create short DVDs with positive sexual health campaigns.

The youth identified issues they face and through storyline development, direction and acting they came up with their own solutions. To date, there have been three Star In Your Own Stories campaigns. The issues they have covered range from encouraging youth to go for STI testing ("rumours and STIs are the two things that spread fastest in a community"), and "coming home to culture". Campaign messages include: Step Up; Don't Stress the Tests; Stand Strong, Stand Together; Own It; Choose the Strong Path, and You're Worth Protecting.

The project is successful in attracting youth to participate and increase their STI and HIV knowledge. Youth reported that it was very educational, fun, and that they want to inspire other youth to learn about the same topics.

This approach is a successful way to involve more community members than would typically attend a health workshop and has a wide reach with positive sexual health and STI/HIV prevention messages. Other opportunities that come with the project include the communities hosting the DVD launches involving more community members; media is also attracted to the project raising general awareness about HIV/AIDS and STIs and also reporting on Aboriginal people in a positive light.

All of the DVDs are available through Chee Mamuk and come with lesson plans for use in sexual health education workshops.

The narrative on the following page documents our journey through the "Step-Up" project and is guaranteed to not only motivate and inspire, but to make change.

* * *

For more information about Chee Mamuk and corresponding programs, please visit: http://www.bccdc.org/content.php?item=96

JADA-GABRIELLE PAPE

Step-Up — A personal narrative

In youth, everything shines. Early morning stretches her arms forever in the sunshine. Dew drops lazily from black branches in the sun, glistening like diamonds. Green moth-like butterflies flit above the green grass, darting toward the windswept, blue sky. Every day has promise; bright eyes, nimble bodies and hair as untamed as butterflies — in youth everything is trouble-free.

There are other things going on in youth too. Alliances are being formed, boundaries being pushed, choices being had and discoveries being made — many of them behind closed doors — the unearthing of adolescent bodies wrapped together, intertwined in the glory of a first kiss.

The "Step Up" youth from Chemainus, Halalt and Malahat are like any other youth today: they are insecure and quick to laugh. They feel safest when they are together. They are beautiful and invincible. They are interested in computers and music and cellular phones. They seem to worry very little about the future; their own nor their peoples. They are in the glorious throws of youth. By dictionary definition they are "the fact or quality of being young".

The dictionary, though, doesn't look at the issues today's youth have to contend with, how each sexual decision impacts their life, how if they avoid making choices or make the wrong choice the consequences can be scary and complex and can shift their world forever. The dictionary doesn't explore the concerns surrounding HIV and STI testing, qualities of a healthy sexual relationship or the realities of peer pressure. These concerns remain uncomfortable topics of discussion; little foreign lands in families that, for multitudes of reasons, parents hesitate to explore with their children.

With every person who tests positive for HIV at least one life, one family, one community, one world is changed forever. The same goes for every person who takes action and gets tested and who tests negative.

These topics are, however, looked at through the *Star in Your Own Stories* project hosted by Chee Mamuk. The discussion about these realities shaped the "Step-Up" campaign. During November of 2006, Chee Mamuk launched a project called *Star In Your Own Stories* and came together with Good Company Communications, AIDS Vancouver Island and a BCCDC Outreach Program. The project was designed to educate youth about HIV/AIDS, sexually transmitted infections, and healthy preventive practices. This education took the form of a three-day workshop process. During the workshop the youth learned about HIV/AIDS, STIs and prevention strategies then grappled with which theme they would present. Later, they scripted and shot their own short video production.

When this thoughtful group of youth first met they were almost completely inaudible when they went around the circle introducing themselves. Their shyness had them almost unable to share ideas with the rest of the group. In only three days, however, this same group, despite their quietness, came up with these powerful positive slogans: Stand strong, stand together; Be strong, stand together; Be your own role model; A decision isn't for anyone else to decide; Best to go your own way; If getting action, take action, take the tests; Don't stress the tests; Own it; and of course their key message: Step-up!

During the second day of the workshop the youth expressed awareness about many issues including the mixed messages we all face about sexuality. The youth observed how the media gives us messages to be sexy, be thin and be attractive while parents give the message, don't have sex or "say nothing". More conflicting messages come from friends and religion: "everyone's doing it" is one message that friends subtly pass on while religion often has people "feeling shame".

For these quiet and shy youth to come together and talk about these wildly uncomfortable topics and then make a short film about them is brave and commendable. "A decision isn't for anyone else to decide". They talked amongst each other, shared stories, filmed each other, forged friendships and, through the seemingly simple act of talking, these youth are changing the world (with all the fantastic bravery and nonchalance of youth).

The voice of the youth carry important teachings and within this traditional style of passing on knowledge comes true power for change. As for the worlds of these youth we hope this project blossoms within them giving them increased self-confidence (because we know how much they have to be proud of). We also hope they come to see themselves as the natural leaders that they are. And of course, amongst the list of goals at the outset of this project, we hope the youth will continue to use the vocabulary, language and teachings and flourish as role models.

The individual decisions of the youth to participate in the *Star in Your Own Stories* campaign tell these youth are good role models. They are part of a hopeful movement towards bringing back artistic expression into communities to tackle history and teachings.

Our decisions about what we believe in and what choices we make are enough to change and shape our world. Our worlds are made up of small moments and decisions: which socks will I put on today? What will I eat for lunch? Which book will I read? Am I ready to have sex? How will I say we need to use a condom? How will I bring up testing for STI's and HIV and when will I get tested? These decisions have the power to change our worlds forever.

If one person sees this film and understands the gravity of their own responsibility to get tested, to make a responsible decision, this film has changed the world. In the context of Aboriginal people and our communities, these decisions will impact the rest of the community. It's not that for us, as Aboriginal people, that our decisions are more important or have more gravity; it's simply that we feel the effects of those decisions quickly — we are inextricably linked to the rest of our communities.

With every person who tests positive for HIV at least one life, one family, one community, one world is changed forever. The same goes for every person who takes action and gets tested and who tests negative. There is again, one life, one family, one community and one world that is changed forever — it's just that we don't know about it. We each have personal control over the small choices but we can't do anything alone. Like the youth said, "Stand strong, stand together". We only have one world. Let's all Step Up to change it.

* * *

Jada-Gabrielle Pape *is Coast Salish from the Saanich and Snuneymuxw Nations. She is a single mother of a four-year-old daughter. They live together in a brown house in East Vancouver with their giant headed pit bull. They all laugh a lot and fall down frequently. You can visit her artistic beauty at: www.jadagabrielle.com*

Say No To Racially Irresponsible Publishing

RENEE MARTIN

Confronting Hyper-Sexuality in the Black Community

As the mother of a young child who is approaching his tween years, thoughtful consideration of our social dialogue as it relates to sex and sexuality has been of great personal concern. Along with assuring that my child receives accurate information to make the correct decisions for him, ensuring that he understands that even the options that are available to him are strictly a result of his race and gender are an essential part of an evolving conversation on sex and sexuality.

When educating black children about sex, it is not enough to speak about the mechanics of the act. Though it is an absolute necessity to stress safe sex in a time where AIDS has reached a truly epidemic stature within our communities, the why we choose to engage in sex can and should be an equally important conversation.

Children come to an understanding of our world by interacting and confronting the agents of socialization. They will receive clear and direct instructions on performing gender, race and sexuality. These intersections are internalized and accepted as normative, despite the fact that they are often damaging on multiple levels.

Black children in particular must deal with the social idea that their bodies are hyper sexual. This can be seen in the overtly sexualized images of black women in rap videos, or the black male as rapist construction. In both of the aforementioned examples, sexuality is perverted in that it is presented as overly aggressive, and existing outside of normalized engagement.

The virgin/whore dichotomy is continually reified through the lens of race wherein white women exist with the construction of purity and the black female is reduced to the ever wanton Jezebel. This construction has its foundation in slavery. It was meant to justify the repeated rape of black women by their white male slave owners.

Though we have long since moved beyond slavery as a condition of living in the broader culture, its shadow continues to interject itself into our discourse about sex and sexuality. Young black girls quickly internalize the idea that their bodies exist for consumption based in the falsehood that they are continually desirous of sex. This construction removes the agency from the decision to have sex and implies that sex must occur because that is the foundation of the black female identity. It further reifies a hierarchy of beings wherein the black female is routinely located at the bottom. bell hooks theorizes that the black woman has no institutional other, and when we examine the discourse of sex and gender what immediately becomes clear is that the politics of colonization and oppression continually manifest in ways in which foster a negative sexual identity in black females.

Reducing black women to simply sexual beings without agency or autonomy over their physical beings translates into high rates of teen pregnancy and a low cultural self esteem. If your identity is based on sexual performance rather than achievement in education, it perpetuates the idea that success can only be achieved by conforming to the role of eternal Jezebel. This creates an unhealthy sexuality in that sex is no longer something one engages in to share pleasure or manifest a loving relationship, but to assert a form of self worth.

While a healthy sexuality is important to achieve a well rounded sense of self, the overvaluation of it is detrimental. Reducing women to what they do with their vaginas rather than with their brains serves patriarchal interests. For black women who have a history of slavery the perpetuation of the Jezebel complex amounts to the continued colonization of black female bodies.

This form of sexuality is also heterosexist nature in that it constructs women as existing solely for the purposes of male sexual pleasure, while ignoring the existence of same sex loving women. Lesbian love is delegitimized because it does not actively serve patriarchy; and therefore its erasure is not only a slight on black women, but on all women that identify as lesbian. Queer culture is very much a part of the black community, but when sexuality is controlled by outside forces instead of individually, certain identities become invisible if it is deemed that their existence does not help to maintain the race/class/gender hierarchy.

Young black girls quickly internalize the idea that their bodies exist for consumption based in the falsehood that they are continually desirous of sex.

The model held for the black male is quite similar to the black female. It once again finds it origins in slavery; wherein the black male was constructed as the sexually aggressive savage to promote distrust between black men and white women. In this way white men are assured their place at the top of the race and gender hierarchy, while constructing themselves as the saviour of white women and the socially evolved masters of black men.

The hyper masculine sexuality that is presented as a model to black men can be seen in rap videos, and throughout mainstream media. The black male sexuality that is offered is one that is desirous of continues conquest; wherein the pleasure of the act itself is over looked. Black men are perceived not to engage in sex because it is an act of intimacy between two beings; rather it is construed as an act that reifies their masculinity. In a world where in the black male is continually reduced to an exotic "other" combating such images can be difficult. If masculinity is derived through sexual conquest, then this reinforces a problematized identity.

Just as same sex loving is detached from black female sexuality, a queer identity is similarly not associated with black male sexuality. Black masculinity is forever measuring itself against that of the white male. Due to the historic imbalance caused by racism any form of sexuality that is deemed "socially deviant" is actively denied. This has given rise to living a life on the "down low". Though black males are certainly not the only ones to lead closeted lives, the tendency to deny sexual orientation is higher because of the association of black masculinity and sexual conquest. This is not healthy and is ultimately damaging to the individual on many levels.

We have a tendency to speak about sex as though it is divorced from other social elements, yet it is one of the most complex forms of human interactions. When we ignore the complexities of race, class and gender in our discussions it has a tendency to minimize the ways in which different groups of people not only understand but experience sexuality. What must be paramount when we seek to educate our youth is that they be made to recognise that though they are the products of social construction, as individuals they exist with ability to transcend norms and create a sexuality that is not only more positive, but a reflection of their right to possess a sexuality in which the onus is on individual agency.

When we begin to discuss sexuality with black children, it is important to make connections to the ways in which racism has affected our understanding of what it is to be black, while at the same time exist as a sexual being. Reclaiming sexuality from the race-infused dialogue would foster a more positive understanding of what it is to be sexual thus encouraging youth to see this as a decision that is not synonymous with claiming their gender identity, but in sharing an experience of intimacy with another.

* * *

Renee Martin *lives in Niagara Falls with her husband and two sons. She currently works as a freelance writer and professional blogger; however the job that means the most to her is wife and mother.*

Our Reproductive Rights!
Right to decide to bear a child or not: to contraception, abortion, self-protection and sex education
Right to perinatal medical care, with full information, and no forced sterilization, no unnecessary Caesarians or hysterectomies
Right to protect children from sexual violation
Right of mothers to justice in custody and family law, including poor, working, lesbian, disabled, battered, and imprisoned mothers
Right of a people to preserve its bloodlines and families, and to survive as a culture
Right of all people to live free of chemical and nuclear poisons that harm our genetic integrity and disrespect Mother Earth
It is a woman's decision whether she will bear a child from her breath, blood, and bone.
Max Dashu
www.maxdashu.net
www.suppressedhistories.net

Coordinated by **ERIN LEIGH**

Canadians for Choice

Canadians for Choice is a pro-choice, non-profit charitable organization dedicated to ensuring reproductive choice for all individuals in Canada. We envisage a world where individuals — regardless of age, ability, race, gender, sexual orientation, place of residence, or socio-economic or other status — have access to the information, resources and services required to make and exercise informed choices on all aspects of their sexual and reproductive health and rights. We work to ensure that the general public, policy-makers and health and education practitioners are well educated and informed about all aspects of sexual and reproductive health and rights. We also aim to enhance the quality and comprehensiveness of research and information on current and emerging sexual and reproductive health issues.

We believe that sexual and reproductive health and rights are central to women's empowerment and to improve the quality of women's lives. When women can control their fertility, they tend to have fewer children, more time between births, and better reproductive health in general. Also, women who are able to control their fertility find it easier to work outside the home, are able to raise their incomes and are more able to fully provide for

Canadians for Choice at the International Women's Day Rally, Toronto, 2008.

their families. They also have more time to participate in the social and political life of their communities. Every year, many Canadian women face the difficult experience of an unintended pregnancy. Since approximately one in five of these pregnancies ends in abortion, it is critical that this medically necessary procedure is continuously being analysed so that it may be provided in a safe and timely manner.

As a pro-choice organization, we want to ensure that individuals have the information and resources necessary to make the right decision for them when faced with an unplanned pregnancy – whether it is to choose parenting, adoption or abortion. Some people think that pro-choice actually means pro-abortion, this is false. In reality, we believe that Canadians must have better access to contraception and comprehensive sexual education so that the need for abortion can be reduced. Pro-choice people do not promote abortion over adoption or parenting. Each choice is valid and each person should make whichever choice is best for them.

In 2007 we launched a groundbreaking research report: *Reality Check: A close look at accessing abortion services in Canadian hospitals* (Shaw, 2007). The national findings show that:

- 15.9% of Canadian hospitals provide accessible abortion services — that is, only one in six hospitals across the whole country!
- Abortion services in Canada are poorly dispersed; the majority of which are in urban areas only 150 km from the U.S. border.

There are a lot of barriers to accessing abortion services in Canada including the barriers of cost and travel to have the procedure, especially for women in rural and Northern communities. We recognize that this is also fundamentally a question of racism, and how the Canadian medical system affects people differently. Intersected with this reality, a major barrier is judgmental gatekeepers.

Pro-choice people do not promote abortion over adoption or parenting. Each choice is valid and each person should make whichever choice is best for them.

In conducting this research, our researcher, who was posing as a pregnant woman seeking to terminate her pregnancy, was hung-up on, laughed at, told that no one would want to talk her, was referred to anti-choice organisations and was told many myths and inaccuracies about what would happen if she terminated my pregnancy — in every province. At countless facilities, she was told "we don't talk about 'that' here." or "try looking in the phonebook under 'A'" before they hung up on her. Sometimes she was directed to Crisis Pregnancy Centres.

This experience led us to look at Crisis Pregnancy Centres (CPCs). These centres advertise their services as supportive and helpful to pregnant women, but often their main goal is to prevent women from having an abortion. There are more CPCs than there are clinics, CLSCs and hospitals providing abortion services in Canada, combined. Check out our website from the end of 2009 for a brief report on CPCs.

In addition to understanding the landscape of hospitals and CPCs, Canadians for Choice has been working on understanding the particular needs, circumstances and barriers facing women from diverse backgrounds. Rather than lumping women into one homogenous category, we're keen to explore how an individual's gender identity intersects with their race, ethnicity, sexual orientation, age, ability, economic status, residence status, and other self-identified strands of identity. Making the connections between a woman's right to choose, and same-sex marriage, for example, lets us explore the fundamental right to bodily integrity.

This work began in November 2007 at an event called "Through the eyes of diversity: reproductive and sexual health in Canada". Speakers representing First Nations, queer, immigrant and other communities came together to talk about choice. This event has cemented our commitment to this work, and we will be applying a diversity lens to future research. We also have a First Nations, Inuit and Métis Committee, which acknowledges the particular historical trajectory of colonization of these communities, and the impact this has had on their approaches to sexual and reproductive health.

Our work to ensuring access to sexual and reproductive health services for all individuals in Canada, including to abortion services, will only be possible if we engage with the day to day realities of individuals' lives — in all of their diversity and complexity. Access is influenced intensely by a person's identity, and recognizing the constraints of marginalized communities, and creating a space for individuals to express and engage on these issues, is essential to making access a reality.

* * *

Erin Leigh *is Acting Executive Director of Canadians for Choice (www.canadiansforchoice.ca).*

ANDREA CANALES

Welcome to Canada

Coming to Canada as an 18-year-old woman robbed me of my sexuality and objectified me as an exotic other. When I landed, my first contact was with an immigration officer who welcomed me by asking if I had come to the country to become an exotic dancer. Within minutes, my skin colour categorized me — all my life experiences and their complexity, the teachings of my ancestors and the pride of my family was erased by that statement, as if I could not be anything but. Would this officer have asked the same of someone else, someone who did not look as foreign as me?

Welcome to Canada. In my new home I am often objectified — deemed unable to control my carnal desires and intent on arousing those of "Canadians" (generally men) who came here before me. Why, I ask myself, do I even have to think about this? Why do I have to carry this burden of discrimination and racism across my back? " Because the colour of my skin connotes that I am "other".

In Canada it sometimes seems that all that I am is a sexual object who has to explain again and again that yes I actually am able to control my sexuality and no, I will not be going home with you just because you asked. My foreignness seems to entitle the same people who treat me as a second class citizen worthy of their pity, to offer me unsolicited advice on what my life could look like if only I would find and stay in my place in society — a place where I could simultaneously cleanse myself of foreignness, while capitalizing on my *muy caliente* personality to attract the right man into my life — instant acceptance!

Upon landing in Canada, my sexuality was no longer mine — my being was predetermined for me long before I arrived. I watch now as comments like the one I was met with on my arrival create confusion and despair among my people, who naturally feel a human need to belong and to fit in. I see the need of our young women to play it cool, to be "hot" and sexy but not different; to "pass", and I see it among our young men who want to be the suave, Latin lover types while struggling to maintain who they really are inside.

The treatment we often get tries to fit us into a box built for us, a box filled with prejudices and stereotypes, a box that we are told to be thankful for, because being in this particular box puts us in the sexual and therefore attractive category. Forget our human aspect altogether, forget who we are as people, forget the multidimensional layers that make us who we are. The need to control us, our bodies and our souls, is a continuing attempt to colonize us because in some eyes we are otherwise worthless. Do you really think that we need to be told what's good about us by those who can't ever know or understand what it is to be us?

As the mother of a racialized girl I'd like to see more than just a superficial layer of education and awareness in our Canadian society. I'd like to see a society where all the aspects of an individual's reality and life are considered, rather than simply considering the needs and preferences of the dominant population.

In the meantime, leave my body, leave my mind, and leave my soul alone. Colonized over and over: isn't it time to be left alone? And please, while you're at it, don't ask me any more stupid questions.

* * *

Andrea Canales Figueroa *is founder and director of the GoGirls, a leadership program in Vancouver, BC, run for and by racialized and indigenous young women. Andrea is the proud mother of a 12-year-old who keeps her on her toes and reminds her daily about the important things in life — reading, laughing, eating, and never, ever giving up.*

Camp fYrefly
A Summer that will last a Lifetime
Join us this summer for fun, friendship, and amazing workshops at Camp fYrefly, Canada's only national leadership retreat for sexual minority and gender variant youth. Please visit our website to apply or to learn how to make a charitable donation to help send a kid to camp!
www.fyrefly.ualberta.ca
British Columbia July 2-5
Alberta July 23-26
Saskatchewan August 20-23
iSMSS
Institute for Sexual Minority Studies and Services

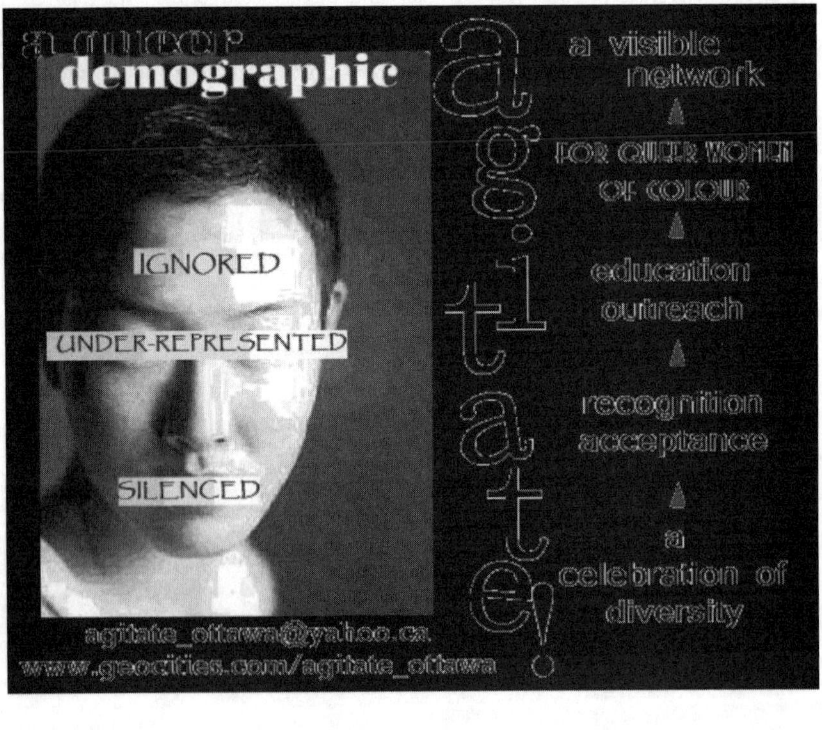
a queer
demographic
IGNORED
UNDER-REPRESENTED
SILENCED
agitate!
a visible network
FOR QUEER WOMEN OF COLOUR
education outreach
recognition acceptance
a celebration of diversity
agitate_ottawa@yahoo.ca
www.geocities.com/agitate_ottawa

"I'm a star on the soccer team,
I'm a straight A student,
and I'm three times more likely than
most of my classmates to attempt suicide...
I'm gay."
Nova Scotia Teachers Union

Ready when you are
Community
College
Teachers
A real degree
of difference
National Union
of Public and General
Employees
www.nupge.ca

Every kid counts!
BC teachers want to give all students the individual attention they need to succeed at school.
That's why we are calling on the provincial government to live up to its promise to address large class sizes and guarantee support for students with special needs.
A message from the BC Teachers' Federation
For more information, please call (604) 871-2283

Point Youth Media (PYM) is a youth run and led grassroots organization determined to make a difference in the way youth are viewed in both the local and global community through the use of art. Its mandate is to use media art to empower and engage youth with focus on racialized youth. As an innovative new organization it will break normalized and institutionalized barriers by having racialized youth at the forefront of organizations, as well as in the media world.

PYM's initial project was named 20 Days Behind the Eyes of 20 Ugandan Children and done in partnership with a local Ugandan organization. It exists under Globart: The Global Youth Art Initiative which connects youth on a global scale using creative forms of media arts. The first phase of this program was done in Uganda, and the second phase will be done in Vancouver, BC. This programming will help build the foundation of Point Youth Media's work.

More information can be found at http://twentyscenes.wordpress.com.

Point Youth Media believes in promoting the positive work done by local organizations by working in partnership with organizations that operate out of our host regions. PYM forms partnerships between organizations which foster and challenge the people within them to reach out to more youth and continually cultivate greater ideas.

Contact Info:
Point Youth Media
pointyouthmedia@gmail.com
http://pointyouthmedia.wordpress.com

Taking Action!

ART and ABORIGINAL YOUTH LEADERSHIP for HIV PREVENTION

www.takingaction4youth.blogspot.com

Art, hip-hop, storytelling and cultural pride
Youth will lead the way to HIV prevention in Aboriginal communities

There is so much in Aboriginal (First Nations, Métis and Inuit) history and teachings that supports healthy sexuality. And Aboriginal traditions have always recognized the power behind the youth voice. Yet there is a huge lack of culturally relevant information about HIV, which affects Aboriginal youth and their communities at sweeping rates across Canada.

It is time for Aboriginal youth to get involved in creating culturally relevant information that educates and helps in the prevention of HIV/AIDS. Unleashing the creative power of youth as health promotion activists is a successful approach, used both in Canada and around the world.

With this in mind, several community and academic partners have developed the Taking Action Project. It aims to involve Aboriginal youth as HIV prevention leaders, using both traditional art forms and new media approaches. Aboriginal youth, with the help of artists and community partners, will tackle the higher HIV infection rates among members of their communities by developing and showcasing their own creative, art-based responses.

This project is about engaging Aboriginal youth, taking pride in our culture, peer-education, and leading the way to stop the spread of HIV! We will work with 6 communities in different parts of Canada over the next 3 years to develop youth leadership and to involve the communities in HIV prevention using the talents of the phenomenal artists we have across our nations.

Please visit our website regularly for updates, progress reports and resources on this initiative.

Partnerships in the Taking Action Project include:

The Canadian Aboriginal AIDS Network
The Native Youth Sexual Health Network
Pauktuutit Inuit Women of Canada
Chee Mamuk

and academic researchers:
York University
McGill University
University of Toronto

ABORIGINAL
STUDENT
SERVICES
We Are Here To Support You
www.ryerson.ca/aboriginal
RYERSON UNIVERSITY

hws yr sx lyf?
I finished my doctorate by age 25 so I could help young adults while I was still young. Now at 27, I teach and counsel clients. Lots of people need help. When you need help you can call me or email me. Set up an appointment to talk about your sexuality more in depth or email your questions. Your sexual health is important to me; I get it. Helping you is my job.
Judgment-free, youth-friendly, really smart.
doctordoe.com
"Montana's only clinical sexologist"